Perspectives in Group Psychotherapy

A group in action! This was the 289th meeting of the Korean Armistice Commission (April 12, 1969). It went on for eleven hours and ended in four hours of total silence!

Perspectives in Group Psychotherapy

A Theoretical Background

by P. B. de Maré M.R.C. Psych.

Consultant Psychotherapist on the
Teaching Staff at St George's Hospital
and at Halliwick Hospital
President of the Group-Analytic Society

London. George Allen & Unwin Ltd
Ruskin House Museum Street

Printed in Great Britain
in 11 point Plantin type
by Cox & Wyman Ltd, London, Fakenham and Reading

To Turid

With acknowledgements to Mr Anthony Barry who
pointed out the photograph for the frontispiece, which
appeared in the *Guardian*, and also to Mr Earl Hopper
whose comments on the chapter 'Sociocultural
Perspectives' proved most helpful; also to Mr Peter Wells
whose comments and corrections of the proofs were
invaluable and to Mr David Mitchell for drafting the
index.

The author and publishers also wish to thank the publishers
of the following works for their permission to quote
excerpts, namely:— Group Psychotherapy by S. H.
Foulkes and E. J. Anthony (Penguin Books Ltd). Sociology
and Modern Systems Theory by W. Buckley (Prentice-Hall
Inc.). Textbook of Analytical Group Psychotherapy by
S. R. Slavson (International Universities Press, Inc.). C. E.
Jung on the present trends in group psychotherapy by
H. A. Illing. (Human Relations and Basic Books, Inc.).
Language in Culture and Society by B. Bernstein
(Harper and Row) and also to the Associated Press Ltd.,
for permission to publish the photograph of the Korean
Armistice Commission.

Preface

As the title indicates, this book is concerned with putting into perspective the theoretical background of group psychotherapy, viewed as an important development in modern times. It represents a very painstaking effort on Dr de Maré's part, an effort which has extended over a great number of years. In this he has without doubt met a deeply-felt personal need. Others who have a similar need will assuredly gain from his work, and should find it stimulating and informative, if not always easy reading.

In his own words, Pat de Maré uses as his guide 'the triad of structure, process and content'. 'Like many such trinities, this has proved, for me at least, a convenient signpost through the morass of detail.'

To my knowledge, this scholarly and erudite study is unique in this field. We are presented with a profound perspective, which stems from first-hand knowledge of the relevant sociological, psychological and particularly philosophical literature. This makes us realize how deeply group analysis interpenetrates with these and other scientific disciplines. For members of these different professions and other professions who are interested enough to read this book, it should act as a catalyst and lead them to a deeper understanding of the meaning of group psychotherapy.

In view of our longstanding friendship and co-operation it is not surprising that Dr de Maré takes the method and theory of group analytic psychotherapy as his model. We first met at Northfield: the famous training centre for army psychiatrists during World War II, which was the home and breeding ground of the first 'therapeutic community', and also the centre for group analytic psychotherapy in a great variety of applications. From the first, Pat struck me as a man with an intense and lively interest in human affairs, with a strong social conscience, and one who practises what he preaches.

After the war we came together again; he was a co-founder, in 1952, of the Group-Analytic Society (London) whose President he is now. Personally I am well content that such various and independent work has come from this group of people. Often such work is of a more specialized, technical kind, or serves to show the importance of group analytic principles in education and other areas. What this book does, on the other hand, is to show us how our individual work has in fact been developing since ancient times. In the past, such work has been heralded, forgotten, then taken up again. At the present time, and for deep inner reasons, it has now come into its own and to maturity.

The present writer was aware that it was of the utmost importance to make group analytic principles operative. People would learn more by seeing them in actual operation than by reading about them. In fact this stimulated work in other areas and gave concerted meaning to what was going on. With a certain amount of hindsight, Dr de Maré is now in a good position to show us that such a movement does not ultimately originate in individual minds in separation, but develops and matures through the needs of the time.

Some of the material that Dr de Maré discusses has been quite unknown to me hitherto. On the other hand, work of which I knew and which has influenced me is not always included. But this is no criticism. It is quite impossible to attempt to be comprehensive and complete. It is far more important – as Dr de Maré has done – to study relevant samples of sources in the different disciplines and to present them in creative integration. He does this equipped with capacities not often combined: he does not write from behind a writing desk. He is an intensive, experienced practitioner of group analysis; it is his daily work in fact. He has, at the same time, theoretical acumen and a deep intellectual interest in the metatheory and the wider and deeper implications of this discipline. The very least we owe to his painstaking work is to read this book with care and to study it thoroughly.

London, February 1971   S. H. FOULKES

Contents

Introduction

Confronted by the vast array of variables and unpredictables presented by group settings, it is not surprising that group therapists tend to work in a variety of widely differing ways. Some for instance, embark on their groups already guided by the map of broad theoretical principles; others scorn theory, approaching the situation with an open mind, and only after having acquired some sophistication do they reflect upon their experiences in greater depth. The following survey, I trust, will be of relevance for both these approaches. It could also be of interest to those working in other fields, for instance in social work, in politics, industry and education, possibly also to those philosophers who seek for orientations in fields where chaos or vacuum would otherwise prevail.

I hope too the book will prove of interest to many others besides, for, after all, we all live in groups. For who else then is this book intended? If truth be told, I suppose it has also been written for my own benefit, for in the course of some thirty years' involvement with therapeutic groups I have felt an urgent need to try and clarify certain themes, to steer a way between the extremes of confusion on one hand or the distortions of dogmatism on the other, and to follow up some of the tenuous affiliations that group therapy holds with certain schools in philosophy.

The background to small groups in psychotherapy is a highly complex one, involving the tracing of ramifications into sociology, psychology and communication theory, to name a few. The weaving of a social dimension into the very fabric of psychotherapy has influenced the whole course of psychiatry and is leading us to the field of social psychiatry and community therapy. It has closed for ever the gap between psychology and sociology – between the solipsisms of one and the massifying effects of the other.

13

The treatment of soldiers in groups during World War II has produced enormous repercussions in the field of both psychology and sociology; not to mention the implications it could have for politics, where a more detailed attention to group principles would bring about a greater emphasis on information flow as distinct from coercive relationships.

It may seem incongruous that therapists devote many years to conducting small groups merely to treat a handful of people suffering from neurosis. It is even more incongruous that politics and matters of high finance depend on decisions made at summit talks barely lasting a fortnight, conducted by strangers who often do not even speak a common language – decisions involving the lives of millions of people and the destiny of the world. To group therapists it has become clear that most groups at this rudimentary stage are only capable of very elementary thought processes.

The foundering of intergroup relationships, the loss of control in the 'dust heaps' of the secondary groups of past civilizations essentially involve matters of group insight, of communication, of size and number, whilst at the same time the alienation of the individual from his seemingly unconscious societal context presses ever more urgently for solution. Already well over a century ago, Marx had pointed out the significant increase in productivity of a dozen people working together compared with that of the same number working separately. A few years later, Durkheim described the isolating effects on the individual of 'anomie' or social disequilibrium. Triplett drew our attention to the 'facilitating', 'dynamogenic' effects of small groups upon the participants, and Simmel remarked upon number *per se* as a determinant of social forms and of the structuring of relationships, upon the centrality of 'belongingness'. About the same time (1902), Cooley made a differentiation between primary and secondary groups; he called primary face-to-face groups 'the nursery of human nature'.

These writers were sociologists; their main concern was with large groups. Only later was there a converging with psychologists towards a scrutiny of small groups. Group psychotherapists took up the subject and, by the very intensiveness of their studies, found themselves not only becoming sociologically orientated but creating a feedback with sociological thinking. Today there is an increasing emphasis on social psychiatry, on milieu therapy, or the therapeutic community – also on community therapy within the social services, not only on the socializing of the individual but on the humanizing of society.

This focus upon the interstices between psychology and sociology led to a scientific no-man's-land. Methods designed for physiology proved inappropriate for problems that were relational. The attempts to advance the study of neurosis in physical isolation had reached a standstill. It was only when Freud recognized the significance of relationship (in the transference) that an intelligible field emerged. Group dynamics and group therapy have extended this study still further.

In philosophy, a similar revolution had already occurred. Hume's differentiation of matters of fact from relations of ideas foreshadowed Cassirer's distinction of 'thing' and 'relation', distilled from modern physics. Husserl, in his phenomenological investigations, recognized the crisis of science in relation to consciousness. Heidegger and the existentialists saw the dilemma of alienation, the hiatus of non-relationship between people. For Jaspers, truth was communicability, reminiscent of the ancients who taught that after mathematics we need to learn dialogue or discourse, 'the supreme science 'as Plato called it.

In clinical psychology the absurdity of 'condemning to the flames' all that could not immediately be perceived, or latterly of remaining 'for ever silent' over what could not be clearly stated, had become self-evident. This was made even more so by the essential paradoxes evident in cybernetics and communication theory where noise, random events, contingency, accidentals, and uncertainty constitute the very substance of developmental processes and change. A deterministic, linear, and strictly logically causal approach disallows the circuitous vagaries of system thinking, of small-talk and conversation, of dialogue and free-floating discussion, in particular of free association and group association which constitute the basis of psycho- and group-analysis.

It is hoped that viewing group therapy from these theoretical orientations will bring new emphases and give added consistency to our understanding not only of group therapy but of psychotherapy generally, for of the latter we know very little indeed.

In the course of formulating the following chapters, a schema of a spirally punctuated framework has been adopted, of structure, process and content. Groups therefore, are presented from the perspectives of a sociocultural *structure*, undergoing processes of communication, which convey *content* or meaning. Meaning, in turn, remoulds the relational culture or 'metastructure' of the group.

Let us turn first then, to the sociocultural background of the small group.

Chapter I
Sociocultural Perspectives

Broadly speaking, as applied to sociology *structure* refers to the spatio-temporal matters of when and where and who, of the framework of selection, size, proximity, frequency, duration, etc., for example large or small groups, primary or secondary, institutions, communities, societies, etc.

The founding members of sociology, Comte, Spencer and Durkheim, were particularly concerned with mapping out these areas, totalizing various entities; for example, Durkheim in 1901 defined sociology as the science of institutions. It is structure rather than process and content that concerns the social anthropologist.

Process refers to the dynamic aspects that become activated both within and between these structures, beginning for instance with the simplest unit of a social act, such as a smile, the bricks of observable behaviour, in so far as the acting individual attaches a subjective meaning to it. Action builds up into interaction and communication, establishing attitudes and relationships; sociology, seen from this standpoint, consists of the study of structures in their interrelationships. In physics the equivalent is the relation between atom and molecule, in biology between cell and tissue. The word sociology is derived from the Latin *sociare* meaning to link or join or share, and has been described as the science of interhuman life. Proximity alone does not constitute a group, 'is not enough to turn a number of different objects into a group' (Sheila Thompson).

Content comprises the meaning, the message, the information conveyed by the previous two categories (within structure, and by process). Essentially, meaning is individual and qualitative. The individual experiences personally the effects of being within the structure and of communication. Every communication reflects each individual in a particular light; every action and interaction establishes attitude, role and relationship between individuals. This results in organization, in constellations of more enduring patterns of relationship, and a sort of network or matrix is laid down. This 'metastructure' emerges as a culture which moulds the structure into various shapes as far as its meaningful or phenomenological aspect is concerned. For the group therapist, this matrix is a crucial feature of groups, as it constitutes the significant bridge between group and individual, and also between one group and another.

Content, therefore, has amongst others the following functions:

(a) It establishes cohesion, coherence, continuity, and holds structure together internally, i.e. it is no longer imposed from without. It establishes enduring systems and transmits cultural features enabling the group, for instance, to continue longer than the life-span of the individuals who compose it.

(b) As metastructure, it remoulds structure. For example, a didactic authority-centred lecture setting may be remoulded in the course of its meetings into a seminar; a coercive leader-centred setting may change to a legitimately authoritative situation; an enforced power constellation may develop into a system operating on information as regulating the energy flow of its actions.

(c) It is meaningful for the individuals who constitute the structure, providing motive, purpose and inspiration, in reciprocally evolving relationships.

The cycle starts then with structures in the form of the simplest units bringing about processes and relationships of increasing complexity, from act to interaction, communication, relationship, laying down a meaningful content constituting the adoption of attitudes, of role, status, and stratification, and returning to a structure which becomes restructured by this cycle of events. It is the phenomenology, the meaning of the structure for the individual, that is restructured by the individual. In group therapy we are interested in the fact that social and personality structure can be treated as important, independent, but interacting, and therefore mutually shaping variables, in a process which has come to be known as 'morphogenesis'.

In no other discipline is the hiatus between the 'One and the many' so clearly seen as in sociology – so much so that it would seem to be to this that the philosophical conundrum primarily refers, namely the dilemma at the interface between social cohesion and individual liberty. Philosophy has always been underscored by society and social conditions. Philosophical and sociological systems are continuously being mirrored in each other; for instance Plato recommended rationalism and, therefore, rule by a philosophic intellectual élite; but Aristotle, who was an empiricist, had a higher opinion of diversified democracy – 'One comprehends this, another comprehends that, and all comprehend the whole'.

In classical sociology the rift showed itself in the two major trends which have been termed organicism (the organic whole), and positivism (or empiricism); alternatively sociologism (or communitarism), and psychologism.

How has science managed to approach society? A firm science employs definitive units of analysis, for instance in physics the quantum, in chemistry the element, in physiology the nerve impulse, but in psychology and sociology there is a vast range of controversial and elusive variables over which neither philosophers nor scientists agree – instinct, for instance – and in sociology an even wider range of variables of which habit, attitude, sentiment, and role are examples. There is a bewildering array of research designs and techniques in data collection. It has even been disputed whether a science of society is possible at all. Can it meet the standards of science as we know them today? Some ask whether, with roots in social philosophy, it should not remain a humanistic branch of study. It might be relevant to recall here that the word 'assembly' is derived from an Anglo-Saxon word meaning 'thing'.

In the development of Greek epistemology the discovery of the rational proof in 600 B.C. separated for ever the new spirit of rational enquiry of philosophy from the traditional religious and superstitious trust in belief. Philosophy now made a swing from structured belief to the process of logic. It established the primacy and logic and mathematical conceptualizing as a first base from which to look at the world. Reason became the ultimate virtue in spiritual strength and manliness, and differentiated Western from Eastern philosophy, at the expense, indeed, of experience of both the outer world empirically speaking and of the inner world mystically speaking.

This was logic (where truth lies within the thought process itself), but it was not science. Sociology, psychology, and the world generally were explored from the standpoint of rational thinking. It took over four hundred years before sufficient confidence was felt to make the leap of seeking for concepts from direct observation, of making a swing from process to content – not from the standpoint, that is, of a rational proof, but empirically in the form of the direct validation from experiment, the experimental proof, a service which performed for science what the rational proof had done for philosophy. It was the British empiricist Francis Bacon (1561–1626), in his *Novum Organum* (1620), Hobbes (1588–1679), Locke (1632–1714) and Hume (1711–1776) who felt the need to study nature anew; they supplied the impetus to rely more on the actual experience of the senses. In 1687, Isaac Newton in his *Principia* finally fused the two major approaches of science, namely deductive and inductive logic, the rational proof and experimental observational evidence, together resulting in a restructuring of thought on the basis of science. This has sometimes been described as the first (Newtonian) scientific revolution of classical physics. Later we shall see how the second revolution of modern physics, in the form of field theory and relativity (equivalent to dynamic processes rather than to structure), focused attention upon the dynamic field or space between charges and particles. This was eventually adopted and refashioned in the group concepts and field theory of Kurt Lewin. It is as if these concepts had to be discovered in nature before they could be seen in human nature itself. More recently still, engineering and cybernetics have added their contribution to sociology, psychology and communication theory.

In sociology it would probably be true to say that the second category of *process* has received greatest attention – particularly the aspect of communication, for social process without communication is inconceivable. As a consequence there have been increasing areas of contact between sociology and psychology. In fact, it was a sociologist, Charles Cooley, who presented us with the first coverage of social psychology in *Human Nature and the Social Order* (1902), and it was primarily the sociologists rather than the contemporary psychologists who became awake to the impact on personality of interpersonal relationships and social roles. It was not till 1921 that the one-time psychoanalyst Trigant Burrow recognized the significance of the interactive matrix of society for individual growth, 'phylic' cohesion. He saw clearly the individual as a 'socius', as part of the larger sociological structure. Small-group psychology, however, did not emerge till the mid-thirties, when for the first time the transition to a complete reciprocation was established in which the emphasis and unit for study was neither psychological nor sociological, neither the individual nor the social group, but their interplay, operating spontaneously and simultaneously and directly in the same framework.

Looking at the historical development of sociology we see that, as an identifiable 'scientific' entity, sociology was first conceived of by August Comte (1798–1857), 'the father of sociology'. It was he who first coined the term 'sociology', 'the queen of science'. With the advent of the scientific era ushered in by Copernicus, Kepler, Galileo, Descartes and Newton, the subordination of philosophy to theology (*credo ut intelligam*) ended, and that of science began; *credo* was replaced by *cogito*.

The Scholastics received their death blow in 1793 when the Jesuits were suppressed and Cartesianism prevailed. To this day, on the other hand, certain philosophers, for instance Husserl and Heidegger, have continued to assert the need for the independence of philosophy from both natural science and religion, and to recommend a return to metaphysical reality. They dispute the autonomous attitude of the scientists and consider that we have yet to grasp the history of philosophy as part of our psychic evolution as distinct from social and economic history (Whitehead). 'There is nothing more necessary to the man of science than its history' (Lord Acton).

Until the nineteenth century, then, sociology had been treated as an aspect of philosophy and theology, and the tendency was to study social facts from a philosophical standpoint, to seek what the major structures of society ought to be, rather than examining them for what they are, as for example in Rousseau's *Contrat Social* (1762), in which he stated, 'I seek right and reason and do not argue about facts,' so that, with all historical time in which to develop, sociology as a science is only about one hundred and sixty years old, beginning as we have noted with August Comte's formulations.

In Comte's time, social cohesion had taken the form of a tenuous attunement to very large groups related not to tribe or feudal lord, nor to city state, nor in fact to any sort of primary, but to the vast secondary structures of industrialization. Professor Lewis Mumford, the American sociologist, terms the phase prior to the Industrial Revolution as the 'eotechnic period', the tribal and feudal period of medievalism. During this time, life was founded first on the structure of the family or tribal unit, and only later on the more adaptable feudal ownership of land. Throughout this phase the position of the small primary group was paramount. Everyone knew his place, his function, his rights, and although there was inequality between the rigidly structured classes, there was considerable interchange and relatively little competition either outside or within the categories themselves. Everyone and each group played their acknowledged role in relating and contributing to the whole. Individuals were conscious of themselves as members belonging to a small social group and not as isolated individuals categorized in a vast, anonymous, industrial class, as occurred later. Even the music was formally conventional, expressing social rather than personal attitudes; for instance, the dignified gentle formality of Mozart, in which every note and phrase seems to express a preordained position, as contrasted with the colossal individualism of Beethoven or the personal anguish of Tchaikovsky.

Although it was the Industrial Revolution which brought about this total dislocation, it achieved, productively speaking, more in a hundred years than in the previous thousand. It is this period that Professor Mumford has termed 'palaeotechnic'. It arose indirectly out of the discovery of coal and iron, which replaced water-power and wood. The new methods demanded greater precision to keep up with the magnitude of production, and therefore the more scientific methods already made available by the new discoveries were exploited to the full.

The new methods also affected the philosophical outlook of the time. As we have already mentioned, Descartes (1596–1650), the founder of modern philosophy, decided that philosophy demanded a new method compatible with the more scientific appraisal of phenomena, and enlisted mathematics and rationalism as being more precise.

The English empiricists, too, led by Bacon and Hobbes, keenly questioned the medieval doctrines of the time, and cleared up countless unverified assumptions. In due course they were joined by Locke (1632–1714), another of the empiricists who voiced a thorough-going mechanical materialism. He postulated that a man's mind was like a clean slate (*tabula rasa*), upon which impressions were imprinted, and that man was, in fact, a machine. From there on, the tendency was to make experience or empiricism the starting-point for the analysis of the world and the mind. Spirit was dealt with separately, being virtually avoided, as a polite concession to the conventional morality of the day.

Biology, too, followed suit and attuned itself to the new ideology of social Darwinism, that is, biological Darwinism applied to mankind, which originated from ideas already described in *The Origin of Species* in 1859. It portrayed evolution as possible only through natural selection and the survival of the fittest in open individual competition, a conflict ideology which gave scientific sanction to the outlook of the industrialists of the time. Kropotkin's *Mutual Aid*, published about the same time, gave ample evidence and support to the contrary view, namely survival is possible only through successful grouping.

Religion became individualistic and liberal and was a matter between each man and his Maker. Poverty, which had been regarded almost as a virtue, became a matter of disgrace, and usury was no longer a sin.

The social sciences, till then matters for theology and armchair speculation only, began to emerge, making use of scientific method as applied by the natural sciences, and the age became the most savagely materialistic the world had ever known. People became isolated and alienated, not so much from each other in personal intimacy as from each other in a social setting.

The philosophy of the eotechnic period was that of the Catholic Scholastics. The philosophy of the palaeotechnic phase, was that of the dualistic Cartesians and puritanism. The short period which Professor Mumford called neotechnic, that of electricity and alloy, can perhaps be said to be best represented by the logical empiricists. Today, in the era that is most urgently and of necessity concerned with socialization, humanization and communication, it is only phenomenology and existentialism that can in any way be said to be adequately representative.

The parting of sociology from philosophy began when it was realized that sociology could not derive its facts from philosophy alone. Already in his *New Atlantis* Francis Bacon, inspired by the Renaissance and the revolt against the Scholastics, and foreshadowing Comte, had envisaged the possibility of a scientific approach to society, a society recognized by scientists. Previously the philosophers appear to have been deeply preoccupied with the concept of society as a whole, and it is fascinating to watch the turn-around, not of sociology departing from philosophy, but of that early dissenter, natural science, scrutinizing the philosophy-steeped discipline of sociology.

From the beginning sociology, as we have seen, was projected on to a philosophical backcloth split by the idealistic tradition of Platonism on one hand and by the tradition of empiricism or positivism (as it was later called) of the new scientific era on the other. The idealistic tradition was characterized by three features in its mode of thinking: firstly, an underlying purposiveness in nature, that is, a teleological concept; secondly, a viewing of social phenomena as integral wholes (which tend to lose this property if analysed), for example nature, society, history; and thirdly, the idea that the relation between the parts is like that between the organs of the body. These notions developed from the Platonic concept that ideas alone are the things which really exist and these proceed from some world beyond the world of the senses.

Modern positivism (as distinct from the ancient positivism of the atomists and sophists) on the contrary, was based on observation, inspired by the empiricism of Bacon. It came into its own with the increase in data provided by the natural sciences (astronomy, physics, chemistry, biology). Stemming from this background it was the first scientific school of sociological thought to become known as positive organicism – positive meaning empirical and organic, referring to the organic whole of society. Initiated by Auguste Comte in France, it was elaborated by Herbert Spencer (1820–1903) in England, and was later re-styled by

Lester Ward (1841–1913) from France, and Ferdinand Tonnies (1855–1936) from Germany.

Comte, born on the heels of the French Revolution and urgently concerned with social and political issues, focused on the structural aspects of society; 'the whole human race might be conceived of as the gradual development of a single family'. 'Organic physics' represented the science of the individual, but Comte was primarily concerned with 'social physics' – the science of the human species constituting an immense and eternal unity which consisted of two parts, namely social statics and social dynamics. Statics comprised a study of order, society being conceived of as the organic structural whole analysable into three elements of individual, family and society. Dynamics represented the process of social change and progress which he saw as progressing through three stages: the theological, the metaphysical and the positive. In the theological phase, people's interpretation of reality was dominated by super-stition. In the metaphysical, it was speculative as it could not be supported by facts. In the final stage, which is 'positive' meaning 'objective', assumptions were replaced by a factual content of knowledge, by 'positive philosophy' which he later termed sociology. Science was evolving in logical sequence, via mathemat-ics, astronomy, physics, chemistry, biology and now sociology. He saw a hierarchy in the sciences: first was logic and mathematics, second physics, third psychics, which consisted of biology, sociology and *morale*, 'the true final science', which we now call psychology. Social psychology was a derivative hybrid of sociology and *morale*, and physiological psychology was a derivative of biology and *morale*. 'Psychic' in its original Greek sense referred to anything which lived.

Comte saw, in the society of his day, an opposition between the dying theological and military trends and the new industrial scientific developments. His political approach was neither liberal like that of his predecessor Montesquieu, nor was it revolutionary as was that of his successor Marx; it could best be described as democratic and managerial. He predicted a future of peace, since war served no useful purpose now that industrialization had arrived; both war and revolution had been superseded. This perhaps reflected a reaction against the excesses of the French Revolution, and was an attempt to fuse the organismic concept of wholeness with the disparateness of positivism. But from the beginning, as implied by its very title, 'positivistic organicism' was stricken by inner conflict – by the totalized idealistic 'organismic' concept of society as a whole structural unity, the 'One', on the one hand, conflicting with the manifoldness of individual experience on the other. Comte tried to resolve this by stabilizing the structure of society on the basis of the family system. He considered the Indian caste system was a paradigm of social stability. The development of progress (social dynamics) was progress governed by the discoveries of natural science, which would proceed smoothly and automatically. The mind he reduced to the level of an elemental Nature, and the passive individual would become subject to the application of scientific methods, a scientific re-organization of society already envisaged in Bacon's *New Atlantis*.

The analogy of the organismic formulation was furthered by Spencer in his postulation of a gigantic synthetic sociology of the supra-individual, already caricatured in the big animal leviathan concept of Hobbes; or at a later date by the 'hyperorganism' of De Greef – this school of thought became known as bio-organicism and, in its attempts to accommodate multiplicity by unity, became grotesque and ridiculous. It has disappeared rather completely, but was to some extent taken over by a psychological analogy, an out-look known as voluntaristic positivism: the empiricism had volun-tary purpose, an approach that has also been called psychologism as distinct from sociologism or communitarism; it has also been called irrational idealism since it treated society as a totality, and was irrational in that it gave primacy to the emotional rather than the rational aspect of the individual. Schopenhauer (society moved by a will to power), Nietzsche (the passionate individualist for whom God had been replaced by the superman), Pareto, Freud, Ruth Benedict, Margaret Mead, Abraham Kardiner, Karen Horney, Eric Fromm, are all said to have had affiliations with this form of positivism. In group therapy H. Ezriel's concept of the 'common group tension' as speaking through the mouths of several members also bears a certain analogy. Voluntaristic positivism is said to have attempted to fuse a politically conservative attitude with scientific method, and to that extent it had affiliations with ideology rather than with science – that is with sets of ideas mediating particular social positions.

In somewhat similar vein was Durkheim's collective consciousness, 'collective representations', with characteristics of hyper-
spirituality, personality, creativity and transcendence – for example,
he argued that thought depends on language and language on
society – thus society produces the basic instrumentality of thought,
which represents a like approach, 'angelicism' as it has been called.
He maintained that the causal primacy of the structure of the social
group which precedes and constitutes the individual and social
change is not directly produced or affected by individuals. His
was therefore an idealistic concept of the social group to which he
attributed a group mind, a group unconscious, not meaningless
but too sweeping to be useful, and which tended to support the
dying concept of social mould. In this way he attempted to resolve
the split by applying individual criteria such as 'mind' to the total
unit of society.

On the other hand he was one of the first to make free use of
statistical method in his interpretation of social phenomena, as for
example in his study of suicide, when he used official statistics. He
stressed the significance of social ties within the group. A loss of
goals, values, relationships resulted in social disequilibrium,
'anomie' as he called it, the counterpart of social solidarity, and in
certain cases played a role in suicide. It was loss of love, of sympathetic acceptance within the lives of others, and not a loss of
material possession that played a primary role in suicide. Suicide
was rare amongst the permanently poor and society had claims
upon us that were far subtler and more complex than had been
appreciated.

In due course various writers developed an anti-positivistic bias,
of whom Spengler, Arnold Toynbee and Sorokin (who had called
discussion groups 'chatterbox groups') are examples.

An entirely different attempt to resolve the dichotomy was
made by the conflict theorists, who began to see the underlying
processes of interaction and relationship, and invoked clash as part
of a dialectical relation *process* of development rather than a
structural fusion. Whilst the organicists described the individual
in terms of subordination to the whole structure seen as a unit, the
conflict theorists described various ways in which an antinomy
occurred between the individual and the whole – that processes of
conflict and resolution were the paradoxical essence of society.

These ideas have a long history dating back to Heraclitus and the sophists, to Machiavelli and to Hobbes: the war of all against all, of self-preservation which renders life 'solitary, poor, nasty, brutish, and short'. People escaped from this dilemma by means of a 'social contract', by a covenant, and it is a contract against their very conflicts which is the basis for society. Hegelianism, Marxism and Darwinism were conflict theory ideologies.

Marx (1818–1883), who more than any other philosopher influenced the nineteenth-century social thinkers, tried to resolve the dichotomy in terms of his dialectical materialism. In this he was influenced by his teacher Hegel (1770–1831), who postulated that phenomena were essentially governed by 'processes' of an internally contradictory nature, rather than by fixed 'things'. Contradiction, he said, 'is the root of all movement and vitality', a dialectic not of discourse and reason and dialogue, characteristic of Socrates, Plato, and Aristotle, but immanent in matter itself, affecting methods of production, social structure, history and mankind in general.

Whilst Comte had described social *structure* as resting on opinions, therefore giving sociology a subjective character, Marx is said to have turned that structure, including the extreme rationalism of Hegel, upside down; for whilst Hegel saw the State as a march of God throughout the world, Marx placed social science on an objective basis, in that he argued on an economic, materialistic infrastructure based also on the *relationship* to the historical development in the methods of production. The motive force, as he saw it, lay in a dialectical process of interaction between supra- and infrastructures. Man is not only made by history; history is made by man. Fromm considers that the solution of this seeming contradiction constitutes the whole field of social psychology. 'Men themselves make their history, but in a given environment which constitutes them' (Engels). This materialistically-based concept (though it provoked his hostility) occasioned Durkheim to remark that it had the merit of introducing the idea that social life must be explained not by reference to the ideas of those who participate in it, but in terms of profound materialistic causes of which the participants are unaware, who therefore themselves become objectifiable phenomena. This was for him a necessary precondition for sociology to become a scientific discipline, implicit

28

in which is a notion of the 'unconscious', and without which cause and effect analysis is impossible. It was perhaps also from this notion that Jung derived his concept of the 'collective unconscious'. The unconscious mind, therefore, was initially a construct derived from sociology.

In marked contradistinction to this attitude was that of Wilhelm Dilthey (1833–1911). He made a radical distinction between the natural sciences and the *sciences d'esprit*, counting the social sciences amongst the latter: 'social facts are only comprehensible to us, so to speak, from the inside'. Methods totally different from those of physical science would have to be used to analyse them, based on a kind of direct intuition, of a more or less effective communion, of relationship and communication. 'We will explain nature; but we will understand the life of the soul.'

Positive organicism and conflict theory are the two oldest schools of sociological theory, and they took shape before sociology had become a respectable, institutionalized, professional discipline. The next stage, that of sociological formalism, represents the first official recognition of sociology as a branch of science, and of this period George Simmel (1858–1918) is an outstanding figure. He was influenced by the realists and by the phenomenology of Kant. He objected to the organismic theory of Durkheim, and the over-structured holistic concepts such as a group mind. Society seemed to him to be a function manifested in the *processes* of dynamic relations and interaction between individuals, which was at the opposite end of the scale from Comte's theory; the true units of society were individuals. He saw society as a process in which individuals interacting with each other in due course constituted a unity. He sought to reconcile the theories of positivism and biological organicism in terms of processes of relationship, interaction, communication and money. In his book *Sociologie* (1908), he pointed out that, as a group increases in size, it has to develop processes or mechanisms which a small group does not need; for instance, aristocratic groups are necessarily small.

He set out to examine not the large social structures of such institutions as states, religious organizations, or systems of stratification, permanent and circumscribed, but subjected the transient, directly interpersonal relationships to sociological analysis – those apparently 'tribal' forms of social interaction which he called 'sociation' as distinct from society. Society appeared to him to be endowed with an existence of its own over and above that of the individuals who composed it, a reality external to individuals, moulding every aspect of individual behaviour and consciousness. He considered, for instance, that money (*Philosophy of Money*, 1900) promoted rational calculations within the processes of social relationships, replacing personalized ties by impersonal, anonymous, mathematized relationships based on abstract calculation, with precise measurement and quantification. Purpose and motive or interest (content) gradually became crystallized through processes of communication into forming generalizations regardless of content, taking on forms, shapes, modes of interaction for which that content attained a social reality which could be studied in terms of structure. He considered it was the task of psychology to collate the 'many' and study the *content* of individual behaviour (drives, desires, instincts). Sociology, on the other hand, abstracted out and analysed the processes of social interaction and relationship which embodied this content.

Interaction, he said, presupposed communication. He constantly underlined the interaction between personality and society. Self-esteem and self-identity were intimately bound up with the individual's attachment to others. Personality, therefore, was never a rigidly bounded system; the 'internal' organization of personality could not be understood apart from the individual's 'external' relationship with others. (Hence, logically speaking, it might be argued that personality disorders were likely to be most amenable to change in the setting of a group.)

What now emerged as a rival school to formalism was one which came to be known as social behaviourism, where the main emphasis was on *content*. Three subdivisions have been described. The first was called pluralistic behaviourism, of which Wundt (1832–1920) was the leading exponent. He was to establish the first laboratory for the scientific study of human actions and behaviour at the Psychological Institute at Leipzig University in 1879. Another was the pragmatic, almost existential, approach of William James, who attempted to reconcile idealism with science by considering only the practical consequences of ideas, which enabled him incidentally to remain idealistic. The third subdivision of this approach avoided large scale structural units for analysis and led to the beginning of social psychology, of which the Frenchman, Gabriel Tarde (1843–1904), is considered to be the founder. This school adopted statistical method, and the process of interaction and inter-relation were widely used to establish an inductive sociology based on quantification.

Lebon (1841–1931) extended Tarde's ideas of suggestion and imitation in relationship to crowd psychology. His contempt of the crowd is said to have been related to his fear of socialism. As an example of quantification, in 1928 Chapin raised the question of measuring social status, which he based on such factors as the items found in the living-room as an index of socio-economic status, for example floor composition, and wall coverings.

The pluralistic behaviourists contributed richly to the develop-ment of sociology and were the strong supporters of empirical and statistical method. Though their central formulae of imitation and pluralistic behaviour were too facile, they did make the first step towards establishing a social psychology and mass psychology for which behavioural actions, namely the content, constituted the main field of observation.

The second branch of social behaviourism has been called 'symbolic interactionism'. Whilst the pluralistic school was con-cerned with mass phenomenal content, the interactionists were more concerned with the smaller units, of ideas of the self, the basic content of the personality in relationship to others. William James made contributions concerning the 'I' and the 'Me', the latter being the social, material and spiritual Me, 'the empirical ego' as he called it, whilst the former, the 'I', was the pure ego, the self as thinker and knower.

By far the most significant contribution to symbolic inter-actionism, as far as group therapy is concerned, came from Charles Cooley, who in 1902 located the primary group as being the basic unit, the recurring element, in all societies, and which he charac-terized by:

(1) face-to-face association
(2) small number of persons involved
(3) relative intimacy
(4) relative permanence
(5) the unspecified nature of the association

Cooley's reference to the primary group, quoted from *Human Nature and the Social Order* (1902), the first modern coverage of social psychology, is worth quoting. He wrote:

'By primary groups I mean those characterized by intimate face-to-face association and co-operation. The most important spheres of this intimate association and co-operation though by no means the only ones, are the family, the play group of children, the neighbourhood and the community of elders. They are practically universal, belonging to all stages of developments, and are accordingly a chief basis of what is universal in human nature and human ideals. Such association is clearly the nursery of human nature in the world about us, and there is no apparent reason to suppose that the case has anywhere or at any time been essentially different.'

The problem, as Cooley saw it, was how to build, how to promote, primary group life, the 'nursery of human nature', out of 'highly dependable human motives'. Any national or tribal society is built up of a network of primary groups, and the theory of the eighteenth and nineteenth centuries, of a horde or rabble of basically selfish and unorganized individuals driven by animal instincts, is a highly distorted fantasy – a view, incidentally, that was shared by the psychologists of the time (Freud for instance), who were convinced that there is a basic dichotomy between man and society, that man is basically antisocial. As we have said, Cooley (1864–1929) was one of the social behaviourist group (symbolic interactionism) and George Herbert Mead (1863–1931), who was a friend of Cooley, shared the same outlook. They were both responsible – Mead as a teacher and Cooley more as a writer (for, though he wrote very little, his books were well written and had a lasting influence) – for the spreading of these concepts through the U.S.A. Together they established a turning-point in social psychology – Cooley in his emphasis on the small group (the primary as distinct from the larger secondary institutions and the masses) and Mead in his emphasis on the content of the small group (namely its psychological aspects, seeing the interactions of men in society in psychological terms) – a turning-point which marked the change from 'sociological' social psychology to 'psychological' social psychology. Cooley considered that imaginations people have of one another are the solid facts of society – the 'looking-glass self'.

Mead's emphasis on the significance of role-playing as a means of communication, as a means of anticipating the behaviour of others, of standard roles, of language and the development through language of an awareness of the self – 'an object to himself' which also 'takes the role of the other' – forms part of his basic approach. Role pattern he saw as one of the bricks of the content out of which the structure of society is built. Mead was also a pragmatist who placed emphasis on gesture and language, using Wundt's method of psycho-physical parallelism: 'a self is possible only to a creature that can be an object to itself'. Role-taking and language were significant factors in the rise of the self. Every item of language carried with it some of the social matrix. He opened up the problem of linguistic structuring in interhuman behaviour and the linkage of personality with the social structure. Both he and Cooley questioned the adequacy of statistical method in the particular way in which it had been used for sociology. Cooley brought in the method of studying the contents of systematic autobiography and introspection.

The impetus to confront and study operationally the interactional behaviour of human relationships in small groups was growing, propelled onwards in particular by the industrial problems occasioned by World War I and by the acute financial crises of the 1920s and early 1930s. In this context the contrasting attitudes of Taylor and Elton Mayo are relevant.

Frederick Winslow Taylor developed the beginnings of what was to become time and motion study. He was one of the first workers to explore industrial psychology, and his approach was based on the atomistic 'physiocratic' outlook of the palaeotechnic era of the Industrial Revolution. Each man, 'economic man', was motivated by 'self-love, the governing principle in the intercourse of human society' (Adam Smith, *Wealth of Nations*, 1776). Society was a mass of unorganized individuals in incessant competition. Psychology was the study of the individual mind motivated by fear or greed, 'the carrot or the stick'. Man was a machine, and mental processes and social relationships had not yet been seriously considered. Mind was a reified biological entity; and social relationships had got no further than a rabble. The Aristotelian concept of man as basically a social animal was regarded as idealistic and was replaced by the pseudo-scientism of a caricature man, an isolated machine driven by the coal of instinct. Obviously the need in that case was to treat the machine properly, and 'speedy' Taylor increased the output of one Dutch worker by four hundred per cent, increasing his wage at the same time by sixty per cent.

Industrial psychology being, of necessity, operational and empirical, immediate and urgent, tended to caricature the machinery of the situation; and, like the physical sciences up till the twentieth century, it diverted scientific attention away from more specifically human problems.

In sharp contrast to Taylor was the work of Elton Mayo. Born in Australia in 1880, he carried out industrial research at Harvard in the 1920s in connection with the General Electric Co. of Chicago, a firm of 30,000 employees. His researches revealed there was something much more important than hours, wages and physical conditions of work in promoting motivation, something which increased output no matter what was done about physical conditions – a realization, in fact, which came as a blinding revelation – that it was the informal organization of relationships between the workers that was primarily significant. He discovered that the worker was primarily influenced by the relationships of primary groups within the work situation, particularly that of the informal relationship with his workmates and the immediate team spirit generally. His 'cow-sociology', as it has since been called, has been criticized on the grounds that he was hyper-empirical, that is, he amassed observations endlessly and he ignored the difference between science and technology. He showed a naïvety as regards the philosophical background of scientific methodology, and generally discounted the economic and political background of industry, its social action aspects. However, he did, industrially speaking, put the matter of the primary group on the map, in saying that matters of status and prestige were central, within these spontaneous, informal primary groups of eight to ten; also that the members of a work group must be dealt with as a group, as a whole; and that these events were central in determining matters of morale, motivation, and output.

Mayo put paid to the 'rabble hypothesis', the atomistic approach of previous industrial psychologists who studied the worker in isolation. He established that output was closely related to the motivation of the members of a working group, and that views changed not so much on rational grounds or on personal persuasion, as through group influences, through the medium of the group rather than through the individual. For example, he confirmed Burke's remark that 'to love the little platoon we belong to in society is the first principle of public affections'. In effect, he confirmed, industrially speaking, the findings of Cooley: namely that the primary group is the instrument of society which, in large measure, determines attitudes, opinions, goals, ideals, and is one of the fundamental sources of discipline and social controls; that what is known as a crowd or mob is entirely different from either primary or secondary group formations, and can only exist in their absence; and that the individual is always related to the larger group, for example, society or nation, through the medium of the smaller and more intimate groupings. It is the primary group that is the basic unit of society. Professor Kimball Young writes: 'These groups are primary in several senses. They are the first group in which the individual builds up his habits and attitudes. They are fundamental to the development of the social self and the moral sense, and give one the basic training in social solidarity and cohesion.'

Another symbolic interactionist whose work on small groups deserves special mention, was F. H. Allport. He described such behavioural features as 'facilitation' in groups, confirming that people tend to work faster in groups. 'The individual in the crowd behaves just as he would alone, only more so.' He talked of social reality, and described such features as belongingness, cohesiveness, reinforcement, effectiveness, and leadership which have since been more widely explored by others, in particular by the micro-functionalists.

One of the most significant discoveries was that the group context materially alters the content of the perceptions themselves, and Gardner Murphy considered the psychology of perception to be the keystone of modern social psychology. Sherif noted that group norms affected perception in ways that could clearly be demonstrated and measured – for instance, the movements of a fixed point of light which is perceived as moving when it goes out.

Asch measured the extent to which there occurred changes of individual opinion to conform with group norms, and the effects of group climate on learning processes – for instance authoritarian and democratic groups. Murphy pointed out the immense importance of size of the group: groups where one is lost, and groups in which one is found. He described groups which were impersonal and mass-like, others in which solitariness occurred, and, thirdly, small groups which were free from either of these disadvantages.

Whilst the pluralistic behaviourists took the triumvirate of sympathy, of imitation and suggestion, and of statistical content as their starting-points, the symbolic interactionists took the meaningful content of interaction and relationships, of attitudes, mutual expectation, language, and social role as theirs – the emphasis being upon the meaningful content of actions and relationships between individuals.

On the other hand, the third category of the social behaviourists – the social actionists – took the meaningful content between the individual and the total social structure or society as their starting-point. The content of meaningful social action was for them paramount. They saw government in terms of socially-meaningful actions. Social action was the ultimate object-matter for study in sociology. Behaviour in relationship to its social meaning was observed and measured in all aspects – from the outside as it were – for its relevance and meaning for the social setting in which it was being enacted. Max Weber (1864–1920) and Karl Mannheim were their leading figures. They conceived society as contained by a network of meaningful individual acts. With the Marxists, Mannheim was convinced that class-based actions were among the most significant in modern times, and he made extensive studies of ideologies.

Talcott Parsons was, in his earlier work, prior to becoming a 'structural functionalist', a social action theorist. He analysed social contents in terms of unit acts, voluntaristically and intrinsically rational, as atoms of society. William Whyte's *The Organisation Man*, David Reisman's *The Lonely Crowd*, C. Wright Mill's *White Collar* and *The Power Elite* represent other examples of this approach.

To recapitulate the main historical trends: Comte saw social development in three stages:

(i) as based on mythical, superstitious, religious, militaristic and fetishistic or anthropomorphic wills and social phenomena which were ascribable to beings or forces comparable to man himself;

(ii) as based on depersonalized metaphysical forces when abstractions such as 'Nature' were invoked – this philosophical as distinct from theological approach to society was initiated by the breaking away of philosophy from theology as symbolized by the rational proof of Thales (600 B.C.);

(iii) as based on facts established by the empirical proof of experiment; the scientific method of observation, experiment and the establishment of scientific laws; the fusion of the rational proof with experimental, observational, inductive evidence as described in Newton's *Principia* (1687), and signposted as the first scientific revolution.

Comte proceeded to divide science into: first, the sciences of inorganic nature (physics and chemistry), which are analytic in the sense that they establish laws among singular phenomena or elements; secondly, into psychics, which are synthetic as instanced by biology, where it is impossible to describe an organ or a function apart from that of the living creature as a whole, structured organic entity. He transposed this primacy of entity over element into sociology, so that one element of social entity was only understood in terms of entity or the totality of society, and one moment in the evolution of this entity was only meaningful in terms of historical time as a whole. For him, then, the structure of society itself *is* the human mind, and the single design of history is the progress of the human mind, alias society. Only society reacts intelligently – men singly act emotionally, and sociological laws will operate by processes as incontestable as those at maths and astronomy. There is no free will in mathematics or in politics, only a unifying principle of consensual agreement between minds. The scientific era begun by Comte was to consist of the study of laws of historical development. He attempted to resolve the dichtomy between the 'one' of sociologism and the 'many' of psychologism by rendering human nature sheeplike and unalterable and incapable of directly affecting the structure of society in any way, representing a dichtomy that has remained as manifest as ever, and with which

37

most sociologists today refrain from becoming too involved. To us as therapists, however, this still remains a crucial matter, since neurosis can be regarded as the outcome of the discrepancy between these two perspectives – social structure and psychological processes.

In psychology the individual is regarded as a unit, as a fact. In sociology the social fact is first and foremost a collective fact of the suborganic facts of the individual. Viewed from the standpoint of today, the attitude of positivism is usually regarded as somewhat intolerant and destructive to the individual. The various attempts by which the dichotomy has been approached have been in terms of the following alternatives:

(i) To regard the collective structures of society as primary and autonomous, and as distinct from the individuals they subtend; the individual is only a derived reality. This is the way in which Comte and the classical period of the positivistic organicists channelled matters. Society moulds human nature. The One here is paramount, One meaning collective; the One *is* the many, beings becoming Being; ontic becomes ontological; existence becomes essence; the many, the individuals, are simply obliterated.

(ii) To do the opposite. Human nature moulds society. The individual is primary as in voluntaristic positivism and psychologism. The One is an individual who takes over in the form of the superman or the small group of an élite; the One becomes one; Being becomes being, and the collective becomes split and hierarchically structured, in that sense losing its collective identity and therefore, as a collective fact, becoming secondary. In the schema of structure, process and content, the structure becomes content.

(iii) To regard the collective as an outcome of individuals who are dynamically related, as constituted of inter-individual, inter-mental relationships in a state of becoming rather than being. This approach was foreshadowed by the classical, political economics of the physiocrats, founded by Adam Smith (1723–1790), who saw sympathy as the fundamental fact of moral consciousness, and all interpsychological transactions in economic terms. Marxism, gestalt psychology, field theory, communication theory, all have in common that it is neither the individual nor the group, neither the part nor whole which is primary, but it is the interstice of intercommunication, interaction and interrelation which play the primary role. Gabriel Tarde (1843–1904), as we have noted, is regarded as the father of contemporary social psychology ('inter-psychology'); he limited the group to reciprocal relations between individuals. He has had considerable influence, not so much in France, but in England and the United States, on people like McDougall (1871–1938), Giddings (1855–1931), and Cooley, and the rationalist Chicago school of George Herbert Mead, where Thelen and Dorothy Stock Whitaker, at a later date, played a significant role in bridging the gap between group function, as such, and group psychotherapy.

Problems arise, however, not only at the interpersonal level, but at the *intergroup* level. At the level of the primary group or tribe (intragroup level), society has always found itself able to cohere, avoiding the anomie of social disequilibrium and of a 'heap of individuals' without links with each other. Society forms a social web in which all smaller groups are intertwined. Splits in the interstices of this matrix result in social disruption and individual instability. One presumes that the potential of the human brain at the level of the cortical network is more than sufficiently geared to accommodate such a nexus of communication, as man, the social animal, the socius. We are assured that the human brain is, as a mechanism, far more intricate than any other.

On the whole, the social behaviourist approach is too general, too crude, too gross, too outward, to be directly appropriate in this context of therapeutic small group analysis. The usual duration of the observations of this school is too short-lived to be applicable. Rather, one might more justifiably reverse the procedure, since the intensiveness of group psychotherapeutic studies offers insights which certainly have significance for sociology. However, from the behaviourist field of symbolic interactionism, in particular such constructs as Cooley's primary group, from the field of industrial psychology (in particular the work of Elton Mayo), from gestalt psychology and from the culture pattern theorists (Fromm, Horney, Erickson), many of whom had personally experienced the full impact of social disruption, arose a school of thought which was particularly apposite in the understanding of these dynamic aspects of the interhuman level, concerning itself with systems of relations in large and small groups, and known as macro- and micro-functionalism. Talcott Parsons broached the macrofunctional

39

theory of personality by linking the two extremists in psychology and sociology, namely Freud and Durkheim, utilizing as the link between them the interaction of two or more persons considered as a causal 'system'. Freud, he suggested, failed to consider the fact that the individual's interactions with others formed a causal relationship or a 'system', and Durkheim failed to see the social system in terms of the interaction of personality. Parsons described various systems which he defined in the terms of systems and subsystems – a small system being a new whole composed of a plurality of interacting persons motivated in terms of a tendency to the optimization of gratification.

Macro- and micro-functionalism have been said to mark a return to positivistic organicism, but this is not a return. Rather, it is a reintegration and a deeper recognition of the close interplay of structure and content, of the one and the many, the whole and the part, as revealed by gestalt theory, in the form of what I have called a 'changing metastructure'. Gestalt theory was inspired by the new concepts and new directions in the theory of thinking – for example the 'inherent contradictions' of Hegel and Marx, by the desiderata of association theory which failed to distinguish sense from nonsense, sensible from senseless combinations, or to account for the productive and creative aspect of thinking; influenced also by the development of mathematical (as distinct from traditional) logic which introduced a study of relational networks (Whitehead, Russell *et al.*) and by the Husserlian 'phenomenological reduction'. The step was taken of relating gestalt theory, not only to perception, to thinking processes, to personality structure, but now for the first time to the social field, in investigating the relationship between group and individual far more rigorously than had been done previously.

It also made the valid distinction of dividing itself into macro- and micro- functionalism, though the gap between the two approaches now appears to be narrowing. Microfunctionalism is particularly relevant to us as group therapists, as it deals with small-group phenomena as instanced by the work of Lewin, Lippitt, White, Cartwright, Zander, Asch, Festinger, Bales, Sherif – all sociologists who made the small group the focus of attention in the light of gestalt theory. They have accumulated evidence to show that the small face-to-face group can be described in terms of properties belonging to the entire relational system of the group, as revealed by the experimental manipulation of such variables as roles, goals, standards, cohesion, communication, patterns, etc.

Kurt Lewin's work in 'group dynamics' (a term he coined in 1939) is said to have changed the course of social science critically and fundamentally. During his professional life of some thirty years, he said that the social sciences emerged from speculative system-building, and went through a phase of extreme empiricism, but have now reached a more mature stage in which empirical data are sought because of the significance they have for systematic theories. The essential nature of the scientist's work consists in making a proper translation from phenomena to concepts. The process of conceptualizing itself contains some of the most critical problems facing the scientist. Lewin was influenced by Cassirer, the philosopher of science, who postulated the basic character of a science as being the eternal effort of going beyond what is regarded as scientifically accessible at any specific time, and which has, therefore, to go beyond 'methodological taboos' in order to progress. In 1923 Cassirer made the differentiation between two modes of theorizing, namely that of 'thing' concepts and that of 'relation' concepts.

Transferring his attention from the individual as a unit for study, and from that of the group, Lewin focused entirely on the elusive problem of the relation of the many to the one, of the interdependence of individual and group, of the ground and figure flow.

'The essence of a group is not the similarity or dissimilarity of its members, but their interdependence. A group can be characterized as a "dynamic whole", this means that a change in the state of any sub-part changes the state of any other sub-part. The degree of interdependence of the sub-part of members in the group varies all the way from a "loose" mass to a compact unit' (Lewin 1943).

The controversial issues of the present day in group psychotherapy hark back to the Cartesian subject/object dichotomy. Psychologists tended to study only directly observable facts, to rule out the study of purpose, to 'scientificate'. The social psychologists on the other hand, less bound by protocol, were prepared

41

to accept less tangible data such as goal-directed behaviour – an essential ingredient in any case in most forms of psychotherapy. They were more readily influenced by gestalt theory ideas, of dynamic as distinct from 'machine theory', and Lewin was influenced by the revelations of modern physics of the submicroscopic units of quantum mechanics, by what has been designated the second scientific revolution. The concept of field theory he borrowed from physics (Einstein and Infeld 1938). 'It needed great scientific imagination to realize it was not the charges, nor the particles, but the field in the space between the charges and particles which is essential for the description of physical phenomena.' The submicroscopic level failed to behave according to established law and could not be grasped by direct perception even with the help of the microscope, but its reality could nevertheless be proved mathematically and demonstrated by the practical application of the formula, as a result of which increasing reliance was placed on mathematics. In the geometry of his 'topology', Lewin showed how mathematics could measure qualities as well as quantities, e.g. in 'hodological space' the path between two points is determined, not by distance, but by attractiveness.

He strongly supported the value of theory ('nothing is so practical as a good theory') pointing out that the organismic formations of the group were not biological entities as such, but could be used productively as phenomenological concepts similarly to the manner in which mathematical concepts were being applied in physics and which were subsequently, often much later, validated by experimental work. He approached such concepts as 'social climate' boldly and compared the relative merits of autocratic and democratic atmosphere in learning processes, etc. He created the 'field', measuring and comparing the demonstrable effects and insisted on putting his hypotheses into testable forms to meet scientific standards. The essential characteristics of his approach were based on gestalt theory, that the group be regarded 'holistically', and that the whole is different from the parts; that the part and the whole interact and effect each other mutually and continuously in a constantly changing equilibrium, but any change in the individual component alters the total gestalt qualitatively; that the part can be seen against the whole in a figure and ground perspective with mutually revealing effects. He emphasized contemporaneity, the 'here and now', that any change in behaviour depended only upon the psychological field at that time. He was influenced by the work of N. Ach (1910), and sought to include goal-directed behaviour, bringing the concept of will into the philosophy of mechanistic associationism, believing that associations by themselves did not provide a motivational force. Thus he transcended the static quality of associationism and also the closely related ideas of Darwin, that directed actions were the result of factors which did not contain the concept of directedness. To avoid teleology, he used less controversial terms such as needs and goal-directed behaviour.

The organismic theories of Trotter, Freud, Lewin and Goldstein differ from each other in terminology, but were not incompatible in the way in which the atomistic, mechanistic approaches of Wundt, Kraepelin, Müller, etc. had been, for there is a coherence of consistent thinking that weaves itself through the ideas of Marxism, phenomenology, gestalt theory, psychoanalysis, and existentialism.

What should be made clear is that many of these writers were primarily sociologists. They were not psychologists, or psychiatrists, let alone psychotherapists. In this context the most Freud committed himself to was to say that 'where a powerful impetus has been given to group formation, neuroses may diminish and at all events temporarily disappear'. This is the crux of the whole matter – whether, in fact, these group phenomena can be harnessed in such a way as not merely to nurture, nurse or socialize human nature, but to bring about permanent radical changes in already pathologically disturbed individuals, with the help of others similarly disturbed; whether patients can receive benefit from each other as well as from a doctor. Has the community therapeutic as well as damaging qualities and if so, can we bridge group function with group therapy? Can group therapy be harnessed to group dynamics? Can group dynamics become psychodynamic?

And over what has been an imponderable enigma since the beginning of time – namely that of the relationship of the one to to the many – over which theologians, philosophers, natural scientists and social scientists have deliberated, what opinions have psychologists to offer in this matter?

43

Chapter II
Psychological Perspectives

Psychology lends itself easily to the tripartite division of structure, process and content. It has been described as a discipline lying on the borderline between the biological and social sciences. Individual and group psychotherapy vie with each other for central place on the continuum between these two disciplines. Psychology is in the invidious position of having to apply piecemeal, empirical experimental methods derived from physiology to idealized human speculative problems that are primarily philosophical. Our unit for study in group therapy on the other hand, is not the 'intradermal' entity of the individual but a unified field of considerable complexity and multiple variables of the socius or of a basically psychosocial unit, whose framework lies around an area containing the biological and ecological, the environmental 'ecosystem', undergoing processes of communication whose content is the psycho-socio-cultural dimension. The problem of motivation has remained inaccessible both to behaviourism and Gestalt theory, but becomes clarified if viewed as a primary feature of a unified theory which includes the social, the psychological and the biological. It cannot primarily be located in any one of these systems, since each one of them plays an essential role.

In the past, the study of the human mind came under the heading of pneumatology. For Plotinus (205–270), all reality consisted of a series of emanations from the One which in this book has been turned upside down to be represented as the psycho-socio-cultural context. The first emanation was called Nous – that of mind or intelligence, the second that of Psyche, soul or spirit, and the third was the most peripheral and concerned matter, sometimes understood as psychic energy, with a divinely inspired part (rational), and a more emotional physical aspect. In early Christian and Gnostic philosophy, pneuma or spirit was distinguished from psyche or soul. Pneumatology began, therefore, as a theological, speculative treatment of spirit and soul. It was not till 1732 that Christian von Wolff first approached the subject in a purely secular sense in the analysis and interpretation of mental phenomena. In the latter half of the nineteenth century its references shifted from the predominantly philosophic to a primarily scientific study of mental phenomena, not as a speculative discipline but as an empirical science. However, to this day the struggle between rationalism and empiricism, between 'mind' and 'behaviour' still continues.

The early psychologists placed their main emphasis on the mechanical structural aspects – the laboratory, the 'brass instrument', empirical tradition of mind in relation to matter, mind-matter monism, the psychophysics of Fechner (1801–1887) and the collection and combination of elementarism, associationism, sensationalism, faculty theory. Then later appeared the statistics of Galton (1822–1911) and the behaviourism of Pavlov (1849–1936) and Watson (1878–1958), who argued that psychology should take its place among the natural sciences. Finally the S. R. theorists, (the stimulus of situation, and the response or act), have followed up this line of thought.

The rationalists on the other hand, stemming from the Scholastic tradition, stressed the process of the mental act as distinct from behavioural content, and emphasized the unity and uniqueness of the ego and self-determination. Their tradition continued through to the early modern rationalists, such as Descartes and Leibnitz, and though Descartes split body and mind, which was quite at variance with the Scholastic doctrine, he helped preserve the mind from mechanism. Whilst the empirical associationists' tradition viewed mind as mechanical, as passive, and divisible into elements, faculties, etc., rationalism saw mind as active and purposive and unitary. Von Wolff (1679–1754), who adopted the triad of cognition, affect and conation, and Hartley, Carl Stumf (1848–1936), Franz Brentano (1838–1907), William James (1842–1910), Husserl, the Gestalt School, Heidegger, the phenomenologists and existentialists, maintained a philosophical hold on psychology – in the form of act psychology, intentionality, and functionalism, in

45

which mind was conceived of as actively sensing rather than as merely being sensed. Husserl and Freud, who were contemporaries, and who both studied under Brentano, and the main body of clinical psychologists continued the trend of exploring a meta-psychology whose content was holistic and personalistic and sought to provide its own discipline and glossary of terms – the total content of mind as such, with its crucial dynamic aspect of motive and purpose, crucial that is, for psychotherapy, the psychology of psychology.

Inevitably the limitation of the insulated, individualized, 'closed' approach was compelled to recognize the presence of interrelationship and its extension into group psychology. The scientific career of small groups can be divided into two phases, a pioneer phase beginning at the turn of the century and a very lengthy past. From the beginnings of recorded time, group methods had been applied for both healing and teaching, for healing by magic, religion or art, for example the healing temple of Epidarus (600 B.C.), the emotional orgies of the Bacchic rites, the catharsis of the Greek plays (A.D. 200), the faith-healing and miracles associated with religion and the Socratic method of teaching by dialogue in small groups or 'schools', by a technique known as anamnesis, of recollection or calling to mind, of remembering. The first person to be associated with adopting a more medically formed group approach was Anton Mesmer, in the early 1700s. He arranged patients round a wooden tub from which iron bars protruded and against which they held the affected part, mentally healed by the animal magnetism he had himself instilled into the apparatus. A scientific commission was set up to investigate his claims. They reported the cures as real but the maladies as imaginary. About a century later the Marquis de Sade, whilst an inmate in a mental hospital, produced plays which were acted by patients for the entertainment of the local inhabitants; he did this to relieve his own ennui. The superintendent of the hospital observed the beneficial effects of these theatricals upon the patients and approved, but the opinions of the medical staff were divided, and several members are reputed to have objected. The theatricals were looked on in very much the same way as psychodrama and encounter groups are regarded today.

In 1904 two French psychiatrists, Camus and Pogniez, published a book, *Isolation and Psychotherapy*. In applying the Weir Mitchell technique of rest and over-feeding and stimulated by the writings of Dejerine, they noted that the poorer patients in the large communal wards at Salle Pinel of La Salpêtrière did better than the more opulent ones treated in isolation in the private rooms. This they attributed to the mutual benefit which the patients derived from each other.

Dr Joseph Pratt (who at one point was taught by the industrial psychologist Elton Mayo), is sometimes regarded as the founder of group psychotherapy. In 1905, he is said to have initiated what Corsini calls the pioneer period of group therapy. As an internist at Boston, he presented a paper at the Medical School entitled 'The Home Sanitarium Treatment of Consumption', which included the teaching of tubercular outpatients by his class method of hygiene regimen including rest, fresh air, and good food. In 1930 he simply transferred this technique to psychiatric patients without involving any other form of psychotherapy, and he found that, as with tubercular patients, it was the sick human being he was treating rather than the disease. He pointed out that the word 'cure' was derived from the Latin *cura* which meant 'care', in the way that a *curé* has the parish under his 'care', and he emphasized that the patient should not lose his personal identity in becoming a patient. His meetings began with a roll-call, and he addressed the group of twenty or more as if talking to a single person. Each patient (quoting from his article written in 1953) gave in a slip stating whether he had improved, whether his condition was stationary, or whether he had not improved. Those who had not improved were given an individual interview. People attended twenty-five to a hundred meetings or more. Pratt was guided by the writings of Dejerine and T. A. Ross, and he quoted Dejerine's remark that 'psychotherapy depends wholly and exclusively upon the beneficial influence of one person or another. One does not cure by reasoning or syllogisms. Patients are only cured when they come to believe in you.'

In 1909 Cody Marsh and Edward Lazell began working with a deliberately revivalist type of technique which they called 'revival – inspirational', consisting of classes of about sixteen people which included patients, relatives, teachers, nurses, clergymen. All enrolled as students (patients included), and had to sign a

47

'psychiatric pledge' to co-operate and to be punctual and regular in their attendances. No charge was made as the meetings took place in the State hospital, but Marsh, writing about it subsequently (1935), considered a charge should have been made. It was never called a clinic but was treated as a mental hygiene class, with the accent on education, on teaching rather than treating. It constituted a sort of milieu therapy – one gathers that the clients were favourably affected by the atmosphere, which in itself was regarded as the therapeutic, and that they sought further individual attention if required. His credo of group therapy was 'By the crowd they have been broken; by the crowd shall they be healed'.

Subsequently he expanded the class into a pre-educational institute in Boston on a paid basis and gave a course of four lectures, in which he included talks on the family situation, on childhood, on jobs, on social, emotional, religious and sexual problems, on the meaning of mental disturbance and the criteria of normality.

Marsh noted that the neurotic patients in these situations became less involved in transference and they tended to put up less resistance to this type of instruction. At the end of the lecture discussions took place in an atmosphere of academic dignity, without the use of jargon and with a certain 'air of sunniness and lightness of touch'. Before and after the class, students were encouraged to be sociable, with flowers and a piano. Rowdiness was ignored, and spontaneity encouraged. 'Hazing' (the equivalent of heartiness) occurred, which was regarded as helpful – it was noted that neither the psychiatrist nor teacher should haze, but only the students. Individual prognosis involving matters of co-operation and improvements was discussed and each student was graded accordingly with a progress card. Students were deputized to help each other, and the class was given various tasks (including homework). Amusements were arranged such as tap-dancing, which was considered admirable as an 'emotional exercise for limbering up'. Informal dramatic groups were arranged, with the shyest person given the role of the gayest social lion. Follow-ups were arranged with the help of student reunions. Marsh pointed out the need for social workers and occupational therapists, etc., but finances did not permit.

He treated all sorts of psychiatric disturbance, including psychotics, stammerers and various psychosomatic and organic disorders.

Stammerers in particular did well, and Marsh noted that language was no obstacle – several members spoke little English (for instance Italians, Russians), but they seemed to derive as much benefit as the others. The classes included people of various levels of intelligence and social strata. Even the simple-minded appeared to grasp what was discussed; the lectures themselves were presented in the simplest language. The psychology of the group appeared to level off many differences, and very shortly the group took on a uniformity of interests as well as of progress. In an attempt to educate the public, Marsh developed large ex-patient meetings on a national basis with local groups and branch bulletins – a liaison which was helpful in problems of rehabilitation and foreshadowed much that has subsequently been more widely developed.

Turning now to the early pioneers in the psychoanalytic movement, the attitude of Adler and his co-workers (which has been described as 'socioteleological') must be regarded in outlook at any rate as essentially group-orientated. He saw the desire to belong as a prime human motivation, that man was a social being who was goal-directed, and these goals were primarily of a social nature. He gave expression to these ideas in a book entitled *Social Interest* which was published in 1920. In 1921 he opened a centre in Vienna, which appears to have been a form of individual therapy in the presence of a group of therapists, beginning on an instructional basis carrying therapeutic implications, not only for the patients, but for the doctors, social workers, teachers and psychologists who attended. Unfortunately the *zeitgeist* of the time seems to have been far more favourably disposed to the developments in individual psychoanalysis, which was perhaps the reason that 'Adlerian groups' did not flourish to the extent one might have expected. One of the pupils, Rudolf Dreikurs, started 'Collective therapy' for alcoholics and later as a method of family counselling, which he brought to the United States in the late twenties. These 'Adlerian groups' also began to emerge in London during the thirties, applying the insights gained from Freudian and Jungian and Adlerian theory in a semi-didactic, semi-interpretative group situation.

Freud and Jung appear to have been definitely antipathetic towards group psychology as such, adopting attitudes which reflected irony mixed with suspicion. They both saw the group as a uniting, massifying phenomenon, and made no clear distinction between small and large groups. Jung's attitude is well described in a correspondence he had in 1955 with the American psychiatrist Dr Hans Illing (quoted from *Group Psychotherapy and Group Function*, Rosenbaum and Berger, 1963). He wrote:

'As a physician I consider any psychic disturbance, whether neurosis or psychosis, to be an individual illness, and the patient has to be treated accordingly.' 'The group *increases the ego*; i.e. the individual becomes more courageous, more impertinent and assertive, more secure, fresher and less cautious; the *self*, however, is reduced and is pushed into the background in favour of the average. For this reason all weak and insecure people wish to belong to clubs of organizations, even to a nation of eighty million.'

He considered that group therapy was only capable of educating the social human being and that it could not replace individual analysis – that a small group, if a good one, could have socially favourable influences. The dialectic process between two human beings was paramount, together with the subsequent intrapsychic catharsis. Since the only bearer of life and the absolutely essential element of any kind of community is the individual, it follows that he and his quality are of consummate importance. The individual must be complete and must endure, otherwise nothing can exist, since any number of zeros still do not amount to more than zero. A group of inferior people is never better than any of them, that is, the group is also inferior, and the state which is composed of sheep only is never anything but a herd of sheep, even though the herd is led by a shepherd with a biting dog.

'In our time, a time which puts so much weight on the socialization of the individual because a special capacity for adjustment is needed, the psychologically oriented group formation is of even greater importance. In view of the notorious inclination of people, however, to lean on others and on isms rather than inner security and independence which should have first place, there is the danger that the individual will equate the group with father and mother and will thereby remain as dependent, insecure and infantile as before. He may become socially adjusted but what of his individuality, which alone gives meaning to the social fabric?' 'When a hundred clever heads join in a group, one big nincompoop is the result because every individual is trammelled by the otherness of the others.'

He went into the poor morale of large organizations, for instance Standard Oil, the Catholic Church, the German Army, National Socialism and Communism.

He summed up by saying:

(1) group therapy is necessary for the education of the social human being;
(2) group therapy does not replace individual analysis;
(3) both types of therapy complement each other;
(4) the danger of group therapy lies in a standstill on a collective basis;
(5) the danger of individual analysis lies in neglect of social adjustment.

In brief, it would appear Jung had considerable misgivings lest group therapy should annihilate the individuation of the 'self', which was based on the antitheses he saw between individual analysis and group analysis – presuming that the principles of each were intrinsically different.

Freud's attitude seems to have been far more complex, as if he were often on the brink of relating group and individual psychodynamics very closely indeed. His view must have been obscured by his failure to consider the *small* primary group setting as such. The fact of the matter was that both Freud and Jung included the collective group unconscious in their formulations but this, it appeared, therapeutically speaking, could only be approached in the clearly defined subject-object setting of individual treatment. He made the statement that '... tendencies inhibited in their aims whose inhibition has not been entirely successful have made room for a return to the repressed sexual aim. It is in accordance with this that a neurosis makes its victim asocial and removes him from the usual group formations. It may be said that neurosis has the same disintegrating effect upon a group as being in love. On the other hand it appears that where a powerful impetus has been given to group formation, neuroses may diminish and at all events temporarily disappear. Justifiable attempts have also been made to turn this antagonism between neuroses and group formation to therapeutic account. Even those who do not regret the disappearance of religious illusions from the civilized world of today will admit that so long as they were in force they offered those who formed them the most powerful protection against the danger of neurosis. Nor is it hard to discern in all the ties with mystico-religious or philosophico-religious sects and communities the manifestation of distorted cures of all kinds of neuroses. All of this is bound up with the contrast between directly sexual tendencies and those which are inhibited in their aims.' 'If he is left to himself, a neurotic is obliged to replace by his own symptoms formations the great group formations from which he is excluded. He creates his own world of imagination for himself, his own religion, his own system of delusions, and thus recapitulates the institution of humanity in a distorted way which is clear evidence of the dominating part played by the directly sexual tendencies' (*Group Psychology and the Analysis of the Ego*, 1921).

Unlike Cooley, who almost twenty years previously had considered the primary group to be the nursery of human nature, Freud shared with the psychologists of his time the idea that there is a basic dichotomy between man and society. Man is naturally antisocial, and neurotics are those who have fallen by the wayside in the drive towards a civilized society, for whereas criminals rebel openly against their society, neurotics do so in secret. Freud was a materialist who for a time tried to convince himself that mental activity could be explained in terms of physics and chemistry. He described his theories as a mythology, and clearly supposed they would be replaced, not by other psychological theories, but by the advancement of knowledge in neurology and physiology. Psychoanalysis was fundamentally a biological theory of personality based on a man's biological nature and upon the theory of instincts. However, the theory of instincts can be used in two very different ways, either as referring to specific and fixed action patterns, which it is generally agreed are largely replaced in man by intelligence and flexible learnt behaviour (and therefore man has no blind instincts in that sense), or as referring to needs, for instance sex and hunger, which have already been investigated by the sociologists: prestige, status, etc. Unable to locate a self in neurological terms, he moved away from these 'process theory', 'natural science' terms, away from the bio-psycho-physiological impoverishment of 'psychology-without-a-self' towards a 'personology' with a meaningful content, however antipathetic he may have felt towards it, indeed as he described.

Both Wundt's and Francis Galton's approaches were flourishing when Freud was a young doctor – they both regarded psychology as a branch of 'brass instrument physiology', (a term coined by William James). For instance, Galton's *Principles of Physiological Psychology* was first published in 1873, when Freud was seventeen, and in these circumstances the realization grew that it was not Freud's terms that tended towards anthropomorphisms but the clinical facts. He made the monumental point that all thoughts, fantasies and dreams have a psychological content of meaning, and were of significance in terms of an autonomous psychological reality which could not be satisfactorily transposed in terms of any other discipline but which, if necessary, could be harnessed for therapeutic purposes by interpretation. Though hidebound to the prevalent physicalistic attitudes, he was, in fact, without fully realizing it, a revolutionary as far as the common scientific *Weltanschauung* of his time was concerned, an outlook which had assumed that biological and psychological phenomena were only explicable if reduced to the terms of chemistry, physics and neurology, of electrical potentials and neuronal interconnections. Foulkes has put it that

'Psychoanalysis does not belong exclusively to the natural sciences, but to the social sciences as well. Dynamic psychology or psychoanalysis needs new criteria distinct from those of physics and the concept of science might have to be changed to do justice to a dynamic psychology which is based on the social nature of man, on the interpersonal nature of the data.'

Similarly, Fairbairn stated that he would regard psychoanalysis as a scientific discipline rather than as a natural science.

In other words, sociology and psychology have difficulties in defining their positions *vis-à-vis* the natural sciences, and also in relation to each other, probably because the natural sciences in particular have adopted an idealized, isolated approach to experience and knowledge, abstracting themselves from life, singling out special aspects which then become lifeless absolutes, and in their hyper-empiricism obviating the necessity of relating to any sort of whole reality, of thinking creatively, often emerging as a cloak for nihilism, a denial of the totality of human experience which in fact should form the basis for empiricism. Freud shared with Hobbes and Lebon a pessimistic view of the masses – libido and aggression are basically 'egotistic' and antisocial, and human nature, which is perhaps another word for the human race, is innately unfitted for good personal relationships, as self and pleasure-seeking rather than object-seeking, to be socialized only under heavy pressure and coercion.

More recent developments tend towards the opposite view, that good personal relationships are not desired only for the sake of pleasure, but are themselves a basic need and that aggression and pleasure-seeking as such in isolation, are the result of splitting occurring from the frustration of this primary aim, (Klein, Fairbairn, Guntrip). Psychotherapy in that case is based on the concept that the primary aim is object-seeking and becomes therefore not only an attempt to relieve symptoms, but is a method of expanding and fulfilling the individual as distinct from coercing, negating and disciplining the 'universal biological man', and should accordingly provide a milieu in which this can best be implemented. This might account for the impression sometimes created that whilst psychoanalysis cures symptoms, group analysis cures people (Balint).

The two halves of Freud's theory, namely the earlier psycho-biological instinct theory and the later psychological analysis of the structure of the ego, involved two different approaches to psychotherapy. In the former, the symptom was cleared up by gratifying the instincts, but created a psychopathic or sociopathic disorder. Alternatively, it was cured by instituting oppressive measures of coercion, creating at the same time a neurotic constricted personality disorder. Thirdly, as a sort of side effect, sublimation could be invoked by promoting more socially acceptable activities. All of these notions have since been questioned (including the oedipus complex, and the latency period), and reviewed in the light of cultural determinants.

It now becomes clearer why sociology was so much in advance of psychology, conceptually speaking, For one thing, it arose out of a response to the pressing industrial problems of the times, for another it dealt with more sharable, less personal, less hidden, less secret problems; thirdly, society could so much more easily be conceived of as an inanimate object, could be looked at impersonally; diabolical acts of 'society' could be studied impartially without personal involvement.

This very anonymity resulted in a feeling of split between individual and society. A dichotomy ensued between the living individual and the reified alienated society – a split which is basically technical rather than scientific or philosophic, and the problem is a technological one of artefacts produced by disturbed systems of communication.

Aggression had been emphasized at an earlier stage by Adler and later by Freud as it had evolved after his formulations of narcissistic libido, when the ego-id dualism of ego and id instincts gave way to the monism of narcissistic and object libido of Eros, a monism which shortly afterwards returned to a further dualism of Eros and the death instinct, Freud's third theory of instinct. The death instinct was seen as a basic drive to eliminate not merely the neuroses of sex, but all the tensions of life itself, by a return to the inorganic state. Few orthodox analysts have been able to accept the death instinct theory (Klein excepted), eliminating as it does the social factor from the aetiology of neurosis and amounting to a complete biologization of neurosis.

Thus Freud's instinct theory of the ego as 'first and foremost a body ego' carries with it a social and therapeutic pessimism, as distinct from more recent trends in psychoanalysis which see the culture patterns as determining the way in which interpersonal relationships are experienced.

However, it was a mark of his genius that at the same time as postulating the death instinct he extended the concept of the ego-ideal to include the super-ego, of which he said that 'Social feelings rest on the formation of identification with others, on the basis of the ego-ideal in common with them'. 'Religion, morality and the social sense were originally one and the same thing'. (*Ego and the Id*, 1923). In *Civilisation and its Discontents* (1930), he pointed out not only the antithesis of instinctual gratification over and against civilization, but (unintentionally) a possible way out in suggesting that culture can only achieve its aim by means of fomenting an ever-increasing sense of guilt.

'That which began in relation to the father ends in relation to the community. If civilization is an inevitable course of development from the group of the family to the group of humanity as a whole, then an intensification of the sense of guilt – resulting from the innate conflict of ambivalence, from the eternal struggle between the love and the death trends – will be inextricably bound up with it, until perhaps the sense of guilt may swell to a magnitude that individuals can hardly support.'

The way out of this impasse perhaps lies in the fact that first, the primary group is not essentially or inevitably anchored to the family group – it is only when it is mistaken as such that neurosis arises; secondly, that civilization for the same reason is not built up of the bricks of family groups but of primary groups – for instance there is an essential difference between the family of personal origin and the family of procreation, and it is precisely at this point that group therapy can be applied.

Freud's ideas were constantly developing, and when he wrote *Group Psychology and the Analysis of the Ego* (1922), his viewpoint was purely psychological as distinct from biological, though he continued to use the family group as his model. (In effect a social group that is modelled on the family group is essentially neuroto-genic.) He made the observation that character traits have the effects of culture in modifying human instinctual dispositions, which led later to a closer definition of ego and character structure by such writers as Wilhelm Reich, Anna Freud, Kris and Hartmann and in due course to the culture pattern theorists (such as Erich Fromm, Karen Horney, Erik Erikson). The mushrooming of theoretical formulations over practical application is overwhelming. A technical hiatus is only too evident: how to apply these insights operationally and therapeutically. Anna Freud considers that therapeutic analysis of the ego constitutes a far greater problem, technically speaking, than that of the id.

There also remained unsolved the problems relating to that of the structure of the super-ego, which became divided into a pre-oedipal, pre-moral sadistic structure which lost touch with outer social reality in a way in which the oedipal, moral (social) ego-ideal does not. Klein carried the oedipus situation back into the first year of life (a view many analysts do not support). Money-Kyrle described two extreme types of super-ego, one based on a persecutory fear of punishment and the other based on remorse of a depressive type: the personality of the first bending towards authoritarianism and tribalism and the latter humanistic. In Melanie Klein's formulation, these early fantasies of the first year of life could not be resolved by anything less than direct interpretation, for they refer to primitive aggressive material of a pre-social biological internal community which concerns purely an inner adjustment of the individual to himself rather than to society or to the external situation such as an (in her view) enlightened upbringing; these social factors cannot possibly reach such an alienating, alienated self and require direct interpretation if civilization is to be saved. Child analysis will have to become as much of every person's upbringing as school education is now. Melanie Klein therefore supported the primacy of Freud's death instinct. Fairbairn, who has been greatly influenced by her in other directions, differed over this matter. He sees all psychology as both individual and social – as inseparable elements in object-relation-ship – and whilst he recognized the part played by aggression, he did not see it in the form of an actual death instinct. He agreed with the super-ego construct of Freud according to which external social agents are organized into an internal psychical institution. Group psychotherapy he sees as ultimately reducible to problems of individual psychology in a group. Many analysts are critical now of the id concept – for example Alexander, Hartmann, Kris, Loewenstein. Fairbairn, for instance, did not see the infantile ego as split from the id, but in terms of a libidinal and anti-libidinal ego, etc.

Alexander (1925) has described the super-ego as an 'anachronism', 'a boundary formation separating the two systems of the ego and the id and dividing the mental system into two parts, an ego in excellent touch with reality and an id quite out of touch with it, "an introjected legal code of former days". Therapeutic behaviour must be directed against the super-ego whose prohibitions function blindly and automatically. Only the ego can remember. The

57

super-ego is and will continue to be the task of all future psycho-analytical therapy.'

This task would also seem to be one to which the group situation recommends itself, one in which group therapy might very well play a crucial role, on the basis that the role and function of the super-ego must surely, in the last resort, relate to society. Freud shared with Jung the belief in a collective unconscious, an archaic heritage appearing without learning in every individual which includes 'not only dispositions but also ideational contents, memory traces of the experiences of former generations'; he supposed there exists a sort of mass psyche and group mind which is the source of these traces, so that the sense of guilt from events occurring many thousands of years ago will still survive and influence individuals living today.

The essential differences between the two are that Freud made no direct use of the group mind or archaic heritage in psycho-therapy, whereas it is basic to Jung's system and psychotherapeutic method (only of course in the individual setting); that although both conceive of collective symbols as in some way inherited with the physical structure of the brain, Jung insisted on this to an extent that Freud did not, for the Freudian concept was quite limited, consisting mainly of certain forms of symbolism such as the 'Just so Story' of the primal horde, in contrast to the vast Jungian collective unconscious upon the surface of which the tiny ego is a mere excrescence. Modern Freudians make little use of the concept and some actively reject it, but it is worth recalling that Melanie Klein came closer to Jungian concepts of primitive symbolism, which occurs at a very early age and seems to infer that the infant has an innate awareness of parental intercourse and other primal events such as those relating to birth and sexu-ality. On either side these theories raise very formidable scientific difficulties.

Abraham Kardiner and Ralph Linton, Roheim, Ruth Benedict and Margaret Mead are anthropologists who have approached anthropology from a psychoanalytic orientation. Kardiner in particular elaborated a basic personality structure in which he developed the concept that personality structure combines cultural as well as psychological features, and that the personality has nuclear and peripheral regions – the nuclear concerning psychoanalytic levels (oral, anal, genital), and the peripheral levels bearing marks of status and role for which there is a greater freedom to make adjustments. Cultures also have their nuclear and central areas resistant to change, and these all represent a more inter-disciplinary approach. The dilemma for the group analyst is just this, that he does not treat an individual and he can't treat society.

A group of psychoanalysts who became progressively more con-cerned with social relationships were the culture pattern theorists, of whom Karen Horney was one. For instance, she founded a 'holistic' school of thought, studying all aspects of living as a single reality, including cultural factors as potent features. She began writing in 1917 and her final volume *Neurosis and Human Growth* was published in 1950. On coming to America from Berlin during the early thirties, she was struck by the fact that 'many neurotic conflicts are ultimately determined by cultural conditions', and that one cannot possibly afford to overlook the fact that there is no such thing as universal normal psychology, and that many features which Freud assumed were instinctual might in fact be cultural. Erich Fromm also originated from Germany and in 1941 he wrote his book *The Fear of Freedom*. He too differed with Freud over the latter's static picture of society and human nature, with its bio-logical bias, but he went further and made an analysis of Freud's theory in more or less Marxist terms – that human nature is a cultural product not entirely explainable in biological terms.

Whilst Freud, Roheim and Klein therefore had tried to describe all sociology in the terms of individual psychology, and various sociologists (e.g. Durkheim) attempted to explain all individual behaviour in sociological terms, Fromm viewed the matter dialec-tically – the two aspects of individual and social process mutually mould and modify each other. 'Man is not only made by history, history is made by man.' (Engels: 'Men themselves make their history, but in a given environment which conditions them.') The significant feature is that these writers are basically psycho-therapists (using the psychoanalytic technique), who nevertheless call upon social agencies as vital factors. They do not, however, add more than insight to psychoanalytic theory; they do nothing towards evolving a new technique to deal with the problem. Sullivan, Horney, Fromm and Kardiner have together formed what became known as the Neo-Freudian School of Analysts.

They were unified in regarding (1) social and cultural, rather than biological factors as basic to the understanding of human nature; (2) instinct and libido theories as outdated, for example the oedipus complex, that the formation of the super-ego, and the oral and anal phases, are profoundly influenced by cultural factors; (3) 'interpersonal relationships' as a primary factor in the production of anxiety, in neurosis and in the formation of character; (4) sexual behaviour as determined by character rather than vice versa.

The significance of their conclusion was that they represented a move away from the psychoanalytic standpoint towards a greater appreciation of social factors. As we have seen, this had already been foreshadowed by the sociologists several decades earlier in regarding the primary group as the nursery of human nature. To cope with this dilemma, it became inevitable that further actual techniques would have to be evolved. They were, and from three main sources, namely, from various of the pioneers of group therapy, from certain of the psychoanalysts, and from developments in social psychology, for instance the microfunctionalists, initiated by Lewin, who also became known as 'group dynamicists'.

Of the pioneers who continued to play a role in propagating the more recent phase of group therapy which can be said to have emerged during the thirties, Moreno must be regarded as the most outstanding. He developed a technique of puppetry and drama in a child guidance clinic in Vienna in 1911, which he labelled 'psychodrama'. In 1921, he developed the idea to the extent of opening a 'spontaneity' theatre for adults and which also came to be used in the treatment of mental patients. In 1925 he brought psychodrama to the United States. No doubt originally Moreno must have been familiar with the writings of the sociologists Cooley (1864–1929), and George Mead (1863–1931), with their concepts of role-playing, but what Moreno did was to apply the concept operationally in the framework of group psychotherapy and psychodrama. His work has been widely followed in the United States, to some extent in France and Holland, but very much less so in England. He is a prolific writer and speaker, promoting world-wide interest in group therapy, a sort of Orson Welles of group therapy.

He developed a special technique of measuring social interaction which he has termed sociometry, which consists of mapping out on a sociogram the significant attraction-repulsion relationships – the likes, the dislikes, the indifferences, between the various members of a group – giving each person three to five choices for instance, based (for example) on who would like to sit next to whom in a class, forming as it were clusters, or 'social atoms', 'the basic unit of a group', in which the individuals are held together by 'tele' – the feeling of individuals for one another, the cement which holds groups together – from the Greek meaning 'far', or 'influence into the distance', a concept not unlike Lewin's and Bion's valency; it would also seem to bear some affiliation with Melanie Klein's concept of 'projective identification'. Needless to say, the drawing-up of such a sociogram, when applied operationally to a large group such as a school, has considerable impact on matters of well-being and happiness and morale of the total group.

It was out of his interest in sociometry that psychodrama emerged. He concluded that people communicate in modalities, namely monologue or self-therapy, dualogue or dyadic, between two people, and drama or group of which psychodrama is the most important example. Therefore he has developed various techniques on the stage which include soliloquy, self-presentation and self-realization techniques, hallucinatory psychodrama of hallucinations and delusions, double techniques employing auxiliary egos, mirror techniques, role reversal techniques, in which a person in the interpersonal difficulty takes 'the other's' roles, future projection, dream and fantasy technique, analytic psychodrama (e.g. the oedipus situation), including variations such as hypnodrama and puppetry. In *Who Shall Survive* (1934), he suggests that next time God pays a visit to the world, it will be in the form of a group.

Many of the pioneer figures tended to impose a sociological framework, concepts borrowed rather from the large units of sociology than from psychology – seen as antithetical structures, a sort of pitched battle situation between the collective situation and the individual. Throughout there is a theme of dichotomy, of society, conformism, social adaptation, of a relatively rigid and fixed framework such as the community, the class, capitalism, the pledge, the stage even, of the collective unconscious, of the primal horde on the one hand and the helpless individual on the other. Freud, for instance, appeared to make no differentiation between

crowds, large groups or small groups, and as he put it, 'the problem was to procure for the group precisely those features which
were characteristic of the individual and which are extinguished in
him by the formation of the group' . . . 'the aim is to equip the
group with the attributes of the individual' (an approach Aristotle
criticized Plato for recommending).

Of the psychoanalysts who played a crucial role in the develop-
ment of an actual technique of group analysis, Trigant Burrow,
Slavson (a psychoanalytically orientated psychologist), Schilder,
Wender (from the U.S.A.), Foulkes, Bion, Rickman, Ezriel,
Sutherland (from the U.K.), deserve special mention, it was the
psychoanalyst Burrow who first coined the term 'group analysis',
and in whose praise under the title of 'A New Theory of Neurosis',
D. H. Lawrence reviewed Burrow's book, *The Social Basis of
Consciousness*, in a 1927 issue of *The Bookman*. The importance of
Burrow's work for group therapists can easily be underestimated,
partly because his style of writing is difficult, partly because it is
extremely advanced; indeed we may still have much to learn from
his writings.

In many ways he reversed the entire face of psychoanalytic
theory – for him 'an individual discord is but the symptom of a
social discord'. 'The psycho-pathologist must awaken to his wider
function of clinical sociologist and recognize his obligations to
challenge the neurosis in its social as well as in its individual
entrenchments.' He described a preconscious, pre-libidinal phase
of development in the infant entailing a primary identification with
the mother, a psycho-physiological continuity with the mother,
termed a 'primary subjective phase' which becomes accentuated
and fixated to the original subjective mode of continuity because it
has not been enabled to emerge, or gain mature social expression
owing to the fact that society is itself neurotic. Noxious processes
are embodied in the customary norm of behaviour, hideous distortions of human values are embodied in the repression, subterfuge
and untruth of our so-called moral codes and conventions.
'Normality' was, in his view, 'nothing else than an expression of
the neurosis of the race'.

He saw the individual as having an inherent capacity for co-
ordination and species solidarity, that neurotic aspects of behaviour
are derived from the affront to this psychobiological unity occa-

sioned by a neurotic society, and that, for instance, incest awe is brought about secondarily as a protest against this violation – since incest is not forbidden, it forbids itself. *Pari passu* with the social neurosis there is a valid integrative matrix capable of integrating individual growth and phylic cohesion; the individual is an organism who needs phylic integration with the larger sociobiologic structure. This represents a significant departure from Freud's concept that antisocial forces are basic in human organization.

Hans Syz has continued to develop the work of Burrow, and considers that we have now reached a stage of development in handling man's sociological predicament actively and constructively, and it is from this historical survey on the work of Trigant Burrow that the foregoing remarks have been quoted in a condensed form. In brief, Burrow saw the real problem of neurosis as the inward sense of separativeness which dominates everyone – the dim yearning for togetherness which he called the pre-conscious state. It is society that is sick and suffers from social neurosis, so that adjustment of the individual involves compulsion to conform to a social image which renders him incapable of making full and undivided responses to the real biological moment thus rendering him neurotic.

He examined the biological instinctive essential 'organic groups' such as the herd of deer or colony of ants or tribe of primitive men bound by an inner organic bond, and contrasted them with social, political, economic, national and religious groups that are wholly superficial and utterly alien from the point of view of instinctive group life, a sort of collective or pseudo-group formation of conventional tradition or authority. Ideas of the significance of this organic principle involving the individuals of a species had already been made familiar to us by Darwin and Kropotkin, and contemporarily by Konrad Lorenz in his concept of animal rituals and the bond. Burrow considered people have an organic, societal, primitive principle of consciousness and he saw the neurotic as merely having failed to integrate in the collective confederacy of substitutes and disorders which most so-called normal people have the cunning to subscribe to, under cover of our arbitrary pseudo-group symptomatology. He conceived of groups of eight to twelve members, talked of a societal plexus of which the patient becomes part in the group discussions.

Later in 1948, another social thinker, Lawrence K. Frank, posed the same point of view, namely that our culture is sick and in need of treatment, in a book entitled *Society as the Patient*.

During the thirties Paul Schilder, Louis Wender, and S. R. Slavson began practising a form of psychoanalytic psychotherapy in the group setting in which the emphasis lies on the individual in the group rather than the group itself. Slavson states that, based on a hunch derived from work he was doing as a teacher in 1911 in classrooms and other settings, he introduced (1934) the concept of the small group in therapy consisting of five to eight children. Slavson himself, incidentally, began as an engineer, then became a schoolteacher. He became interested in psychoanalysis, which he began applying as he saw it in the activity groups of children. Group psychotherapy had its beginnings with the introduction of the small group, he states, and it is only in a small group that the free associative cathexis can occur, where valid interpretation can be given and telling insights can be acquired. Yet he appears to see the group as such as being untherapeutic and it is only by its very particular handling that it can be employed therapeutically.

In his *Introduction to Group Therapy* (1943) he says, 'By and large it is an error to speak of the group as an entity in therapy. It is always the individual and not the group as such that remains the centre of the therapeutic attention.' 'The greatest single therapeutic value of such groups is the very absence of group formations.' Such formations, he considered, lead to cohesiveness or fixity in the group and defeat the aim of therapy. According to him, transference in the group is multilateral. This means that it is directed towards a number of different people at the same, and at different times. The experience of negative feelings belongs intrinsically to the course of treatment. In the manner of psychoanalysis he sees his group in terms of the initial family group with parent and sibling, and identification transference. The transference to any one individual is reduced in intensity, diluted by the group situation, yet the total emotional feeling is multiplied and intensified by it.

Later, in his *Textbook of Analytic Group Psychotherapy* (1964), he also wrote:

'The therapeutic process by its very nature is antagonistic to group formation and group dynamics.' 'In therapy groups, individual reactions are explored and interpreted in terms of interpsychic determinants in each patient.' 'A therapy group, however, is a conditioned reality, planned and structured by the therapist with a therapeutic aim in mind and a concern with the group's suitability for the participants.' 'No non-therapeutic group could survive long if its members were to reveal their unmoral and immoral acts, fantasies, preoccupation and anger, past and present, as they do in psychotherapy. Nor would such groups hold together if their members attacked and abused one another as they do on therapy. No social–educational group could survive under the impact of free catharsis. The cross-currents of hostility would inevitably cause deterioration and disintegrate it. Nor could a social or educational aim-directed group withstand the uncovering and interpretations of hidden motives and latent meanings which are not always the noblest or purest in nature. . . .' 'As a result group dynamics in therapy groups are automatically nipped in the bud, for just as soon as responses are analysed and related to individual emotional sources they no longer operate for the group as such. It is this process in therapy groups that prevents the emergence and operation of group dynamics manifested in non-therapeutic groups. Therapeutically directed exploration, uncovering, and insight, also prevent group synergy, which demands accommodation of the participants to it. Thus, *the therapeutic process, by its very nature, is antagonistic to group formation and group dynamics.*

Reinforcement of feelings and the intensification that periodically set in, if they be permitted to run their course, do result in specific dynamics. In analytic therapy groups, however, this is prevented by the intervention of the therapist and by his and other members' interpretations, thus dissipating the building up of group patterns and group effort. By their very nature, therapeutic groups favour interpersonal interaction, rather than group patterns.'

'Synergy' is the term Slavson gives to group cohesion. 'This element is absent in therapy groups. In fact its presence prevents therapeutic gains for patients.' Cohesiveness, then, he sees as a destructive force to the individual in the group. (Later workers, Dorothy Stock Whitaker and M. Lieberman, for instance, consider cohesiveness may work either constructively or destructively.)

The emphasis is on the effect of the group on the individual and not so much on the effect of the individual on the group. The dynamic mechanism refers to the individual rather than to the group, and the group is made to serve as a background for any one person in it – softening or intensifying the responses.

Two psychoanalysts already mentioned were associated with initiating group therapy during the thirties – namely Louis Wender and Paul Schilder. To begin with, at any rate, their techniques were didactic and they adopted a psychoanalytically orientated approach. Wender, in 1930, at the Hastings Hillside Hospital, employed a formal lecture type of setting with six to eight patients. He introduced lecture material, with illustrative examples, and leading questions followed by discussion of the answers, but with minimal interchange between the patients themselves, though there arose, to an interesting extent, self-revelation over the matters discussed. The meetings lasted one hour, two or three times a week, and the method did not preclude the continuance of individual treatment.

Schilder's groups, which he began in 1936, were smaller (two to seven), but he too structured the discussions; they started off with studies of the case histories of the group's members, and an elaborate system of questionnaires, followed up by a freer type of discussion which, in an article he published in 1939, he described as 'so-called free-association'. One forms the impression that he stressed the relationships and interactions between the members rather more than Wender. He specified the value of group treatment for patients suffering from social anxiety (shyness, blushing, etc.) and from the obsessional neuroses.

Both these approaches were relatively didactic, with introductory talks concerning such subjects as the conscious and unconscious mind, the significance of dreams, early infantile traumata, reaction formations, repression, rationalization and sexual development, subjects which were put in elementary terms with simple everyday illustrations, adapted to the intelligence of the members. As the meetings proceeded, the theoretical nature of the discussions tended to become more spontaneous, and members showed a greater readiness to discuss personal matters in relationship to the theoretical material. As we have said, Schilder talked of the inter-action between patients and noted with interest the remarkable reaction of one patient to the transference of another for the analyst.

Throughout the thirties interest in small-group work was in the air both in Europe and in the United States. John Dewey's concept of situationism from the twenties ('Conduct is always shared; this is the difference between it and the physiological process'), had begun to spill over into education and social group work, for example Alcoholics Anonymous, which was started by an alco-holic physician and a New York broker in 1935. One should not overlook the fact that the value of occupational therapy and social activities had been appreciated well over a century ago, but in psychiatry it did not receive the recognition it deserved. For instance, St Bernard's Hospital did not open its first whole-time occupational therapy department till shortly after the 1914–1918 war. Joshua Bierer launched the first officially recognized thera-peutic social club at Runwell Hospital in 1938 for acute neurotic and psychotic in-patients. Also throughout the thirties in London and other places, lay practitioners organized discussion groups based on Adlerian ideas, Adlerian groups as they were called. The concept of group psychotherapy, then, was very much in the air during the thirties, though the literature was limited and it was not till the late forties that the holocaust of publications first began appearing.

Slavson, Schilder and Wender did, however, begin publishing their experiences during the thirties. They all lay considerable stress on the psychoanalytic orientation of their approaches. Schilder and Wender assumed the primacy of theoretical under-standing in their groups, using the group situation secondarily to relieve isolation, alienation and guilt. The prime mover in that sense was the analyst in a didactic role, and the knowledge was primarily of a psychoanalytic quality. Slavson, similarly, as we have already seen, whilst much appreciating the potential power and impact invested in the group itself, considered and still considers the cohesiveness of the basic integrating force that ensures the survival and achievement of ordinary groups (which he terms synergy) as preventing therapeutic gain for the patients and as actively anti-therapeutic, and recommends as far as possible that this should be absent in therapy groups. The positive value of the group situation in that case would seem to be, from his point of view, its present value rather than its action, or results, its potential and controlled reality-testing character rather than its actuality, which has to be rigorously controlled by the therapist, in order to use it therapeutically and to prevent its potentially destructive or neurosis-perpetuating features, 'analytic *interview* group psychotherapy', as he calls it: he sees it as a direct derivative of his view of individual psychoanalysis. He began with activity group therapy with children, which, again, he saw as a direct extension of individual play therapy, and there was activity catharsis as opposed to the verbal catharsis of the analytic interview group psychotherapy – non-verbal action interpretation based on the therapists' expressed reactions or his abstention from such expression. The group in that case is essentially leader-centred throughout its career from start to finish.

Alexander Wolf comes of the same school of thought. He began practising groups in his private practice in New York in 1938, but did not begin to publish his findings till 1949. He undertakes what he terms 'psychoanalysis in groups', based on the four basic tenets of psychoanalysis, namely dream interpretation, free association, analysis of resistance and transference, divided into six phases, beginning with first, the introductory or preparatory phase, which may require initial individual interviews (anything from one to a hundred, usually ten to thirty); secondly, the dream interpretation and group rapport phase; thirdly, the 'going around' free-associating phase, in which each patient free-associates about the rest; the fourth phase in which resistances are analysed, for example the transference of a patient 'in love with' the analyst – the compulsive missionary spirit, the various over-rigid defensive roles adopted, such as voyeurism, going blank or silent, hiding behind other members, irrelevant biographies, the treating of the group as if it were a cosily inhibited family situation, etc. He points out the close relation between abnormal social behaviour and abnormal sexual behaviour. The fifth phase, and closely related to the fourth, is the identification, analysis and resolution of transference as it emerges in the group. He considers this the most important work of group analysis, since it repeatedly interferes with the patient's true estimate of reality. The sixth or last stage he calls the phase of conscious personal action, free of transference investments and counter-transferences to other patient's transferences which thereby allows for a true social integration, and a lowering of anxiety or increased toleration for it, which is promoted by group support.

He points out that these six stages are inevitably blended one into the other and that there are really no stages at all, certainly no sharp demarcations, and there is an explicit recognition of the fact that therapeutic powers are invested in figures other than the officiating therapist. Each member is encouraged to see the role of the analyst in a psychoanalytic sense.

Despite his very considerable emphasis on the group as such, he appears to have failed to recognize the possibility that psycho-therapy in a group setting can be primarily conceived as going beyond analytic concepts. He does not deny group dynamics, but gives it a negative secondary derivative significance rather than an essential primary factor of group therapy. In fact, he says, 'the group *qua* group cannot become the means by which its members resolve intrapsychic difficulty. The need for such differentiation led us to change our concepts of the psychoanalysis of groups to that of psychoanalysis in groups. We do not treat a group. We must still analyse the individual in interaction with other indi-viduals.' He shares, then, with others the tendency to relate all group therapy to a psychoanalytic base, the tendency not to go beyond the interpersonal level into the realms of the transpersonal, as Foulkes terms it.

In their later writing, Wolf's and Schwarz's approach to group therapy represents an advance in the sense that they place more dynamic reliance on the presence of the group itself. For instance, by 1950, Wolf had instituted a technique after twelve to twenty-four meetings of one and a half hours each two or three times per week, of supplementing these by alternate meetings in which the therapist did not attend. Despite this his group remained leader and family-centred. He emphasized the importance of the in-creased opportunity for people of ventilating their feelings toward the therapist during these alternating sessions, and of 'the new permissive family' that the groups come to represent for each person. Its constructive effect lies in re-creating the family – but 'with a new look', by creating a permissive atmosphere in which mutual tolerance and regard can flourish. The earlier prohibitive character of the original family is projected, but with less intensity and therefore more easily dispersed.

'Perhaps one of the most valuable aspects of group analysis is that it facilitates the replacing of the ideal of a relationship to the single parent analyst. Instead of offering the questionable shelter of a private relationship with an omniscient ideal, it represents the patient with a group with whose common aims he may align himself. Whereas the basis of private relationships may well be evasive of social reality, and tend to create an aura of isolation, his group acts in just the opposite way . . .' '. . . it poses the ultimate of group association which helps him to realize his full potential as a social being . . .' '. . . helps to destroy the false antithesis of the individual versus the mass by helping the patient to become aware that his fulfilment can only be realized in a social or interpersonal setting . . .' '. . . group analysis is a balance between self study and social study. Their dynamic interrelation reveals and promotes the whole man.' He sees that in a patient's ability to analyse and dispose of his own transference investments lies the ability to establish a final stage of 'conscious personal action and social integration'. (*Psychoanalysis in Groups*, by Wolf and Schwartz, 1962.)

One can oversimplify the matter by a caricature schema to the effect that the early analysts (Wender, Schilder, Slavson, Wolf and Schwartz) practised analysis *in* groups; others, somewhat later, (such as Bion, Ezriel, the Tavistock Clinic generally), practised analysis *of* groups, and finally Foulkes has developed a technique of analysis *by* groups (group association and group matrix), in which the group itself becomes the apparatus for undertaking its own therapy.

More recently during the sixties there has been an enormous burgeoning in the development of other techniques. Most of these have underscored some particular aspect of the previous more orthodox approaches, and some are not concerned at all with the therapy of patients as such but with the developing of sensitivity, of experience, personal growth, and 'mind expansion', with encounter between people generally, and tend therefore to be without institutional backing or medico-psychological implications; rather they are concerned with the breaking down of stereotyped convention and social maladies, often with the inference that it is society which is sick. The range of techniques is enormous and can again be looked at from the viewpoints of structure, process, and content.

As far as structure is concerned there are the changes in duration that have been applied by workers such as George Bach and Elizabeth Mintz in their time-extended Marathon groups consisting of seven to fourteen members, and ranging from non-stop meetings of anything between twenty-four hours and four days.

Other structural changes have involved membership of up to sixty adults ranging widely in age and socio-economic and educational background. These 'workshops in self-understanding' undergo fifteen-week courses of weekly sessions of two hours each, reminiscent of Cody Marsh and Edward Lazell's mental hygiene classes. Malamud and Machover are representative of this technique and owe much to Carl Rogers's views on self-discovered learning in therapy and education.

As far as process is concerned, in certain quarters the currency of exchange has been radically altered in favour of non-verbal communication, e.g. action, acting, playing, games, physical contact, relaxation, massage and oriental philosophy, Yoga, and mysticism. Stimulated by the gestalt therapists, in particular Dr F. Perls, the Esalen Institute in California have evolved a vast array of techniques, and their encounter groups go by a number of names such as human enrichment, human awareness, sensitivity, sensory awareness, personal growth, human relations training groups or T-groups, non-verbal, experimental, body dynamic, sensory awakening groups. Carl Rogers has described this intensive group experience movement as the most rapidly growing and most significant social invention of the century.

The more orthodox and traditional group therapists may look with considerable reservation upon these loose, non-institutionalized proliferations. However, they have only themselves to blame for having initiated the group view of psychoneurosis in the first place. What was intended for psychological purposes only has taken on sociological implications. The subculture has burst upon an open-ended social structure left gasping by these realizations, not least the medical profession, who are in danger of being by-passed. Yalom suggested that probably more troubled individuals seek help from these new groups than from more orthodox sources. Be that as it may, a more playful 'ludic' approach is being adopted which may account for the fact that less catastrophies occur than might otherwise have been expected.

Considerable interest in the Esalen Institute's programme has been evinced by the lay public and the more articulate patients in this country. In any case, many of the ideas were initially suggested by such writers as Aldous Huxley, and Alan Watts in the first place; also by the writings and work of R. D. Laing, who has always exerted an important influence in this field of development, particularly in relation to his work on schizophrenia in hostels and the family matrix. His concept of the direct transfer of 'sets' in the mathematical sense from a past matrix of an extended family group to a present group matrix is very apt indeed. In certain instances where this cannot successfully be achieved and where the missing member of the family cannot be substituted, or projectively introjected into the new situation, a hallucinated figure may have to be created.

In relationship to content some techniques have re-directed the free-floating discussion of traditional group therapy towards certain themes – in gestalt therapy for instance, deliberate 'games' situations are set up and discussed – Dr F. Perls has been mainly responsible for this approach. Dr Eric Berne in his transactional analysis directs attention towards certain patterns of relationship in particular those of the roles of parent, child, adult. Ruth Cohn has done similar work amongst groups of therapists studying the reflection of the transference – counter-transference relationships as described by the therapists concerning their patients within the group of therapists itself. She has extended this technique to management relationships in industry and to inter-racial themes. Her first theme-centred interactional workshop was instituted in 1955.

All 'T'-group and study group developments are essentially content-directed and as such differ from the free-floating group-association which is so crucial and characteristic a feature of group-analytic psychotherapy. Although Kurt Lewin, psychologist, Gestaltist, first started training or T groups as long ago as 1946, there has been a tremendous expansion of this technique since then into the field of education, industry, religion, psychotherapy, social work, leadership training, inter-racial relationships, and penal institutions in recent years. It is also perhaps prophetic that this first training was for community leaders – businessmen, labour leaders, school teachers, to deal more effectively with inter-racial tensions. This nascent field spread rapidly to education generally. What was new in these group studies was the inclusion of awareness of, and sensitivity to, emotions and feelings, personal relationships, and insight into the here and now contemporaneous nature of the group itself – the 'group dynamics' – in addition to the task with which the group is involved.

In the United Kingdom similar developments have taken place, mainly in connection with the work of the Tavistock Clinic. The Tavistock Institute of Human Relations was incorporated in 1947 and has since developed to an enormous extent, to a large degree separate from the Clinic though housed in the same centre. They sponsor a multidisciplinary approach involving service, training and research. In individual, group, family psychiatry, social work, marital studies and Community Mental Health they work closely with the Clinic but in social studies involving large organizations and industry, anthropologists, sociologists, economists, case workers and many other disciplines are involved – the approach is problem-centred rather than discipline-centred. They study human relations in well-being as well as in breakdown and conflict.

An excellent account of the work is given in a publication titled *The use of Small Groups in Training* (1967), containing papers by Gosling, Turquet, Woodhouse, and Miller, which formed the focus of a conference in 1964 which discussed the current approaches being developed by the staff of the Tavistock Clinic and Institute. These describe the study group work involving small groups of general practitioners, post-graduate, social workers, probation, and penal system officers.

As distinct from the T-groups of Lewin, the emphasis is not only on the 'here and now' but also on the 'there and then' regressive forces which constantly obtrude into the otherwise productive functioning of the group. Gosling for instance, reports that the weekly general practitioner seminars took two years before he could feel the members were ready to include lectures in the seminars. The obtrusions concern not only therapeutic problems of the individuals concerned but upsurges of group processes or archaic determinants. The work has to a great extent been based on the pioneer work of Klein, Bion, and Balint in connection with such concepts as object relations theory, work groups, group therapy, and the basic assumptions.

In a monograph in Educational Research, Mrs M. L. Johnson Abercrombie expands the ideas she introduced in 'The Anatomy of Judgement' and points out we do not yet know which is the most effective and economic setting for teaching, whether the lecture, the seminar, the tutorial, or the small group, but it would seem that the latter should be given a higher priority if the general trend is any indication.

The most important work, however, it seems to me has yet to come – namely the application of the T and study groups to large groups and the politico-economic sphere.

Chapter III
Philosophical Perspectives

The basic *structures* of Western philosophy were created by the ancient Greeks. They laid down our framework to epistemology, the 'prior philosophy', as a necessary though interdependent preliminary to logic and to any metaphysical speculation. They proceeded to develop the dynamic *processes* of logic whose demarcation from epistemology is fairly clear-cut, and is the formal science of the principles governing valid reasoning – the form in which we think rationally rather than the things we think about. *Logos*, the word, bears affiliations with our ideas about communication. Out of these dialectical antinomies emerged meaningful *content*, essentially an ontic psychological matter which goes beyond physics – namely metaphysics – 'a science of the soul possessing an inner coherence'. *Cogito ergo sum* defines a meeting-point between epistemology – the study of the nature of knowing, and ontology or metaphysics – the study of the nature of being.

Much of the obscurity of philosophy becomes more meaningful in the light of psychology and sociology and of small group dynamics in particular, since this directly involves the relationship of one to the many, of translating Being to beings, of relating the ontological to the ontic, of phylogeny to ontogeny.

The triad of structure, process, and content has, like so many such trinities, proved (for me at least) convenient as a guide-line through the morass of detail. Practically speaking, these three categories offer a wide but coherent range of possibilities from which to choose when the group convener finds himself at a loss in a confusing group situation. Over group structural matters he is most active, since it is he who structured the group in the first place. Over processes of communication he behaves more as a catalytic agent and is therefore less active, while over matters of content he intervenes least, rather he waits for the shape and therefore the meaning of the metastructure to emerge, about which he can comment and make interpretations.

Theories concerning the relationship of the one to the many, between the cosmic oneness of wisdom and intelligence, and the plurality and diversity of individual things seen everywhere, are as old as reflective thinking. The ancient concept of *logos* denoted reason or order in better words and things as in discourse and mathematical ratio; it constituted the source of all human law and regulated all physical processes. The supreme Idea of Plato, the World Reason of the Stoics, conceived of the world as a cosmic unity, perfect in the adaptation of each of its parts to one another, and of each to the whole. The Stoics thought of the virtuous life as a relation of the soul to God, and Aristotle saw it as a relation of the citizen to the state. *Logos* was seen as the bridge between the one and the many, both theologically and politically; it was the principle that brought back the many to the one, and man back to God. In Christianity it is the Saviour of the world. Sociologically speaking, it referred to the bridging between social cohesion and individual liberty.

In philosophy One is not a number, but is the unity of conceptualization of the idea as distinct from the multiplicity of sensory experience, which paradoxically is also singular, individual, unique and isolated, one as distinct from One. The ancients sought unification and wholeness in contrast to the chaos of sensory experience, for the latter was both chaotic and isolating, and the unity of consciousness and ideas provided a cosmic synthesis for the manifoldness of experience.

The One was conceived of as an independent whole, it was seen in terms of Being as distinct from beings and human beings. Except by mystics, the One is rarely declared a fact of sensory experience; on the contrary, its transcendent, abstract nature was stressed. In the past, sociology and psychology have been cases in point, for either they have shown a tendency to evade relationship by concurrently splitting into abstractions, ideologies, grand theories and system-building on the one hand, or alternatively, they have become abstracted and lost in a confusion of hyperempiricism. It is possible that all relationship and participation may be conceived as dangerous, since the closer and more direct relationships become, the more liable is aggression, eroticism, or emotion to be aroused, and the basic problem in human terms has always been how to relate one to One, without either annihilating one, or creating chaos for the other. Controlled and regulated aggression is regarded by the biologists as a valuable survival characteristic in that it ensures protection of the group and group cohesion – this refers in particular to controlled intraspecific as distinct from interspecific aggression. It seems to be both necessary and undesirable at the same time. The undesirable elements can be deflected, controlled, and taken up in displacement activities of various kinds. Indeed, one definition of society goes so far as to describe society as 'an organization capable of providing conventional competition'. Bond behaviour, ritualistic manifestations of appeasement, gestures of brotherly love, dispersion by territorial distance, hierarchical structuring and manipulations in terms of number and size all represent ways of assimilating aggression productively rather than destructively. We are told it is likely that primitive man roamed the earth in comparatively small groups of fifty to sixty people, and many societies, namely, feudal society, were based upon restricted clusters presiding over small areas of land. The word ritual itself is derived from the Greek, meaning number (as in arithmetic), and one can see a progression of controls from direct aggression to talking about aggression, to myth-making, to ritual, to reason, to logic, mathematics, and science. All involve communication, how to establish and maintain an overall network of communication between the one and the many. Communication alias *logos*.

Bertrand Russell describes the position of philosophy as being intermediate between theology and science, for it is both speculative and scientific, both metaphysical and critical. Alternatively, it can be regarded as it has been by Whitehead, as entirely critical, as the science of science itself when it criticizes method, organizes and gives syntax to the particular branches of science in relation to each other. Being in a sort of no-man's land, it runs the gamut of being either too theoretical and speculative, or too empirical. Science by itself, however, as distinct from scientists, does not create hypotheses, rather it assesses them in the light of the evidence once they have been postulated. When it comes to discovering anything new, there are still no rules other than that of using one's own powers of creative thinking. Mathematics, for instance, says nothing about the world, about external experience, whilst physics on the other hand does nothing else. Although the findings of physics have been widely (sometimes too widely!) confirmed by experience, without the speculations of mathematics in the first place, it could not have existed at all.

Experience by itself is silent; it requires hypotheses to give it a voice. Nature is not a book which we have merely to read when we do science. It is the scientist, not the facts, who speaks. 'Chaos does not organize itself into any cosmos. We need viewpoints.' (Myrdal). Later we shall see that this has relevance for us as group therapists, since group processes are not automatically therapeutic, and it is the therapist's function to discover and employ those that are. Every group is a fresh experience, a new discovery, and unless we approach each meeting with an open and creative attitude, which seeks fresh things, our therapy becomes constricted and stereotyped.

Rollo May has remarked that:

'Every form of psychology or psychiatry rests upon some kind of philosophic presupposition. The only error is not to be aware of these assumptions; the only illusion is to deny them. The presupposition underlying most forms of psychiatric and psychological approaches in the nineteenth and twentieth centuries, is the traditional dichotomy between subject and object formulated by Descartes, the father of modern Western thought, some four centuries previously. This dichotomy was assumed by Freud and practically all other scientists and philosophers of the late nineteenth and early twentieth centuries, despite the fact that this assumption was so much in the air of modern thought, that they who used it were generally quite unaware they were assuming it. Phenomenology and existentialism consist precisely of an attack on this dichotomy.'

Today, the life sciences and physical sciences are becoming clarified in their relationship to each other, and are tending to converge rather then diverge. The gap between scientific explanations and causes on the one hand, and understanding and meaning on the other, is closing, 'the message is the medium'. Russell remarks that while physics has been making matter less material, psychology has been making mind less mental. Particularly in the group situation does this dichotomy – the subject/object dichotomy – lose its significance when observer and observed are seen in a continuous state of mutual interaction and exchange.

Charles Rycroft in an essay 'Causes and Meaning' sees psychoanalysis as a semantic bridge between science and biology on the one hand and the humanities on the other, 'something *sui generis* which could not be fitted into any of the traditional categories'.

In small discussion groups one sees something analogous operating in the spontaneous associations of 'group association' from member to member, for this process not merely constitutes an *objective* (intersubjective, consensual) basis for making interpretations and giving explanations, but these associations are themselves interpretations, *subjectively* based on an 'unconscious' understanding of each other. This is fundamental to the issue of subject/object dichotomy. In the group setting the subject is also simultaneously the object of observation, is also the instrument with which to observe, and in any case a science which is objective and independent of man is now regarded by physicists as a metaphysical illusion in the best traditions of medieval idealism. Changes are brought about by the intervention of the act of observation itself. Heisenberg's 'uncertainty principle' (1927) receives added support in group therapy in such intangible matters as group atmosphere.

Helen Durkin, in her book *The Group in Depth,* gives an excellent account of the controversial issues of present-day group psychology and of group psychotherapy in relationship to philosophy dating back to Descartes, the 'grand philosopher of the new scientific outlook' and 'the first great Renaissance psychologist'. She points out that his formulations resulted in the great flowering of scientific knowledge freed from the dead hand of Scholastic philosophy, a period which constituted the 'first scientific revolution'. The hallmarks of this new science were analysis, measurement, quantification and experimental verification, and ruled out the study of purpose and all facts not graspable by sensory perception. Only those directly observable were regarded as real and worthy of investigation.

Some three hundred years later, signs of discontent with this mechanistic philosophy became apparent, particularly in the realm of the social sciences with their less tangible date such as goal-directed behaviour to account for, with the result that sociology had to extricate itself from this dilemma by going its own way. Psychology on the other hand strove to be 'scientific', thereby sacrificing its most interesting and uniquely human aspects in favour of quantification. However, the initial high hopes for the experimental empirical method of such workers as Helmholtz, Weber, Fechner, Wundt and Titchener began to wane. The philosopher Brentano shifted emphasis from structure to function, from substance to process. He postulated his concept of intentionality which was taken up by Husserl, who developed phenomenology, the empirical study of subjectivity itself, which in turn was taken up by the gestalt psychologists, Wertheimer, Kohler, Koffka and embodied in Kurt Lewin's topological psychology.

By the second half of the nineteenth century then, the shortcomings of the classical mechanistic approach based on Newton's first units of the submicroscopic were becoming obvious, and an increasing reliance on mathematics resulted. The physicist Max Planck's formulation of the quantum theory (1900), which reconciled corpuscular and wave theory, postulating that energy travels in discrete units, provoked a re-thinking of terms amongst the philosophers of science, for example Cassirer. This was followed up by the Einstein's photoelectric law in 1906; and finally in 1916 Einstein – 'the greatest scientist since Newton', – produced his general theory of relativity, and worked on his 'unified field' theory, which he completed in 1949, on the relationships between matter and field – mass and energy – field theory being defined as a detailed *mathematical* description of the *assumed* physical properties of a region under some influence such as gravitation and electromagnetism.

The relevance of this for the psychologists has been to pave the way for the investigation of some of their intangibles which, like electricity, can only be demonstrated by their effects. Russell puts it that 'electricity is not a thing like St Paul's Cathedral, it is a way in which things behave'. This new approach has been described as 'the second scientific revolution'. Man stands somewhere between the world of the macrocosm and of the microcosm, the 'tiny terrible field inside the atom', where the division between subject/ object, observer/observed is no longer definite or precise. Factors that first led physicists to assert their faith in a smoothly functioning mechanical universe, led them to the unseen, unperceivable realm of intergalactic space. Quantum theory, dealing with the fundamental units of matter and energy, and relativity, dealing with space, time and structure describes these phenomena in terms of mathematical relationships. Physicists neither ask nor answer questions of why; objects are the sum of qualities which exist only in the mind, and therefore only as constructs of consciousness. The newly discovered want of determinism in the small-scale world of the submicrosphere is governed by statistical law, by the approximations of probability, in the manner that a statistician can predict future changes in the population as a whole but is unable to predict what each individual will do. This gave the lead to Lewin to use analagous models in formulating his concepts. Freud had only the first law of thermodynamics to work with, the classical mechanics of Newtonian science – the conservation of energy. Lewin, on the other hand, lived in an age in which concepts of systems in tension, field theory, and the second law of thermodynamics were familiar knowledge.

So it now appears that it is not only in the realms of philosophy and psychology that the age-long conundrum of the one in relationship to the many confronts us. What makes itself clear, is that it is the relationships themselves – in the microsphere – that are central and that the uniformity of nature only remains deterministic in the macrosphere. In the realms of psychology, as at the submicroscopic level, the Leibnitzian principles of probability and simplicity have to be invoked. With the individual person the variables are so immense that predictable and precise causal theory has had to give way to probability theory and mental constructs, at which point physics becomes as unknowable as psychology.

As pointed out by Cassirer, it is remarkable how most of the hypotheses occurring in modern philosophy were first conceived of by the ancient Greeks. They created philosophy, with its offshoots of logic, ethics and physics. It was in their mathematics (as an extension of logic) that the Greek genius really showed itself, for they reasoned deductively from self-evident axioms, and tended to avoid reasoning inductively from what had been observed, probably as a result of insufficiency of facts. It is this that has led to the reciprocally unfortunate rift between philosophy and science. Scientific method, though it was the Greeks who first had inklings about it, seems to have been alien to their nature. In fact, it arrived through a lengthy series of developments, starting off from fantasy, magic, myth, folklore, astrology, alchemy and rituals and going on to more organized religion, to the religio-philosophical, and finally to a parting of philosophy altogether from religion. The first endeavours in scientific method are said to have taken place when Thales, about 585 B.C., established a rational proof deduced from a theoretical mathematical premise, namely the measurement of the height of a pyramid, by comparing its shadow with that of his own. Thus was established the first practical utilization of deductive logic, starting from a theoretical proposition and deducing a practical fact. Thales is said to have been the first man to have expressed his ideas in logical and not mythological terms.

Unfortunately, in the reverse of this method, that of induction, of inducing a hypothesis from a collection of empirical facts, the leap from observation to speculation, though postulated as part of Aristotle's logic, was delayed in application and was not effectively established as a method of investigation till some 2000 years later, when Francis Bacon (1561–1626) pioneered the first logical systematization of scientific procedure. He is described as the founder of modern inductive method, the whole basis of his philosophy being practical. He held that philosophy should be kept separate from religion – that the former should depend solely on reason and the latter upon revelation, a doctrine known as 'the double truth'. This went far beyond, and indeed was an attack upon, the Scholastic concept of viewing man from the three aspects of *anima* animal, *animus* mind and *spiritus* spirit which, like the id, ego and super-ego of Freud, were not regarded as isolated entities, but merely as facets of being, similar to the categories of affect, cognition and conation under which all mental processes are often classified, equivalent to affect, thought and motivation or volition.

In *Novum Organum* published in 1620, Francis Bacon described his method of induction as that of seeking *all the available facts*, organizing the results in a systematic way, and observing the connection between them so as to deduce a hypothesis which could be tested experimentally. He recommended the use of instruments such as the microscope and telescope to extend the collecting of facts and observations and further empirical information with which to start off a new cycle of events. He was the first, therefore, of a long line of scientifically-minded philosophers, Descartes, Newton, Hobbes, Locke and Hume, to name a few, who kept alive the mind-body dichotomy that held sway for four centuries and had been subsumed in the mechanistic medicine of Freud's time, and is still a central problem and a hotbed of contention in modern psychiatry. The reason for referring to the matter yet again is that I consider we may find a clearer way of seeing things in the light of the small-group situation, in whose dimension so many dichotomies seen in these other settings are proving to be artefacts, for example 'introvert' and 'extrovert'. In the group one member's introversion is simultaneously another's material for extroversion, so that two events from the individual viewpoint become aspects of one event from the group viewpoint. As with relativity in physics, events occurring in the same place at the same time result in the substitution of space-time for space and time. Thus as Carnap points out, the problem, like all philosophical problems is syntactical and when errors of syntax, that is of arrangement of the context, of the grammar and method are avoided, the problem is either solved, that is non-existent and artificial, or alternatively is insoluble.

The small group is a new and highly significant arrangement, in which relationships of events are studied in the same context simultaneously, with the result that explanations of cause, the 'how' of things, occur concurrently with understandings of meaning, of reason and the 'why' of things, and the dichotomies of understanding and explaining, of identification and of objectification (which mostly means consensual agreement), lose their disparity and are seen as aspects of the same event; the mind-body, matter-spirit attitudes can be dropped as irrelevant in this particular arrangement. One man's behaviour being another man's experience may be regarded as two antithetical events, but if seen in interaction as a relationship it is one event without which the other events could not have become observable, describable facts. This seeing requires the presence of the third person; hence a

83

group, it seems reasonable to suppose, is a group of at least three, for what is a meaningful experience to one person, is behaviour as seen from the outside by a second person. To the third person there are two sets of behaviour taking on a certain pattern through their interaction, relationship and communication, which can be described, explained and understood by a third person in terms predominantly of the other two, as aspects of a single event. For instance, a psychologist interviewing a married couple together may understand the meaning of their behaviour more fully than if he interviews each person separately in the dichotomous setting of the dyad, and he may understand the meaning not in his own terms of experience, but in terms of measurable behaviour between the couple. In other words, whilst in the dyadic situation, one cannot see one's own behaviour, so that meaning and experience become split from behaviour (for instance, one cannot describe one's own pallor). In the triad the split loses much of its subject/object starkness, its bifocalism, and with this its relevance. Behaviour in one context takes on different meanings in another. Though one may well deny that the small group is a self-propelling entity independent of the individuals who comprise it, one cannot deny that it is an extremely special arrangement.

Geulincx, a Dutch disciple of Descartes, circumvented the mind and matter problem as follows. If mind and matter cannot interact, as Geulincx considered, the explanation of their independence could be explained on the basis of the 'two clock' theory. That is, if two perfectly timed clocks are placed together so that one showed the hours and the other chimed them, and you saw one and heard the other, you could think the one caused the other to strike. So it is with mind and body. This rather bizarre explanation nevertheless caricatures many dichotomous concepts. By imposing the artificial dichotomy of this dyadic setting on all settings, these ideas arise as self-evident, but replace the two clocks by two people who do interact, replace mirrors by people in relationships to and communication with each other, when their interaction and communication rather than the separate individual becomes central, then meaning and behaviour become part of the same continuum, if observed by a third person (namely in the triad setting).

Bacon was the first to emphasize the importance of induction over deduction. He attempted to improve on induction by simple enumeration, but failed to do so, and his method is faulty through insufficient emphasis on hypotheses which he considers, like Carnap, should become self-evident through the mere orderly arrangement of data. What in fact seems to happen is that this hyper-empiricism, this multiplicity of facts, creates chaos and general bewilderment. Isaac Newton's attempt to do away with hypotheses altogether – quite apart from its sheer dreariness – has proved singularly unrewarding. Hypothesis – some deductive thinking, in other words – is a necessary preliminary to the collection of facts since, as Russell remarks, the selection of facts demands some way of determining relevance.

However, no one can deny the enormous importance of the empiricists' contribution in creating modern science. The delay in the spirit of empirical investigation has been attributed to the human, ethical and social preoccupations of the idealist tradition of Plato and Aristotle, and although the rational proof of the classical Greeks for ever separated theology from philosophy, mathematics was not given independent status enabling it to become the fundamental tool of science till some two thousand years later, with the appearance of Galileo and Newton.

The career of mathematics, which today is involved in the study of language, has indeed been a strange one. Ever since Pythagoras (532 B.C.), considered intellectually to have been one of the most important men who ever lived, 'the Son of the God Apollo' (alternatively the son of a substantial citizen of the island of Samos), created mathematics in the sense of demonstrative deductive argument, being at the time intimately connected with a peculiar form of mysticism, there has been an opposition between those who thought science was mainly inspired by mathematics and those who were more influenced by the empirical sciences. Plato, Aquinas, Spinoza and Kant belong to the mathematical party, while Democritus (the founder of atomism), Aristotle and the modern empiricists from Locke onwards, belong to the opposite party. The latter failed, therefore, to give the language of mathematics, which was to become a fundamental tool of science, its due significance, and it has only been recently, with the development of modern logic and analytic empiricism that a significant rapprochement has been made between deductive and inductive reasoning, between mathematician and empiricist. This approach has called itself the new philosophy or realism, and has not yet reached a final form. Essentially, it regards philosophy as being one with science. Planck, Bohr, Heisenberg, Russell, Carnap, Frege, Whitehead, Winstein, are amongst the names who have contributed towards this approach, which has given rise to the theory of relativity and to quantum physics, and has also revealed the imperative need for a logic of language.

Although the Greek idealists and the Scholastics have been held responsible for this delay, the truth is that they had access to far fewer facts, and we might well take a page from their book in the assiduity with which they concerned themselves with social philosophy. For instance, Aristotle wrote a series of monographs on the constitution of 158 foreign and Greek states (of which unfortunately only the Constitution of the Athenians survives). From the first, they were concerned with the relationship of the one to the many, a problem as old as reflective thinking. They sought the ultimate building blocks of the universe and of its contents, including man. They hoped to understand better the complex entities by a knowledge of the atoms or elements of which they were supposed to be composed, but above all they studied such matters as individual liberty in relationship to social cohesion.

This concern for the individual in his community might have borne some relationship to their geographical conditions. Since Greece was a rocky, mountainous, infertile land, famine and scarcity were never far away. The people therefore tended to cluster round the more fertile valleys close to the coast. Little separate communities grew up, each centring round its own city, usually a port or near a port, with the sea on one side and the agricultural valley on the other, as with Athens, Sparta and Arcadia. When the populations outgrew their surrounding resources, either the inhabitants took to seafaring, or broke off and set up new communities or colonies. Compared to the despotic rule which prevailed in the Egyptian or Babylonian civilization, where a divine king owned all the land and ruled with the help of an aristocracy, the social structure of these small Greek communities could afford to be affiliative and democratic because of their size. They were ruled by their own citizens (women and slaves excluded). The structure, therefore, was that of the *polis* a city-state built up of family, household and village units: psychosocially speaking, it was a highly sophisticated and productive primary group situation, which from a psychiatric viewpoint was healthy and produced human beings who were vigorous, hardy and creative.

Had each state been able to resolve its inter-group problems with other states, to combine together instead of claiming absolute sovereignty, this magnificent achievement might have grown from strength to strength instead of succumbing to mutual destruction and finally to the Roman conquerors. The internecine Peloponnesian War saw the end of the city-state. The people lost their freshness and freedom of thought and lapsed back into nihilism, cynicism or religiosity. In this connection it is interesting to note that Rome, too, began as a city-state.

In this context it is important to realize the size of the polis. Plato ordained that his ideal city should have five thousand citizens, and Aristotle stipulated that each citizen should know all the others by sight, similarly in fact to Cooley's description of the primary group. He implied that many Greek poleis were too small, for many had less than five thousand, that a polis of ten thousand would be impossible because of non-self-sufficiency, while one of a hundred thousand would be absurd (equivalent once women and children and slaves had been subtracted to the size, let's say, of Birmingham), because it would not be able to govern itself properly. In fact only three poleis reached more than twenty thousand, and Sparta, which covered a relatively enormous area of land, could be crossed by a good walker in two days. Religion and political thinking were intimately connected within the polis, which came to mean the whole communal life of the people, political, cultural and moral.

From the time of Homer's *Iliad* and *Odyssey* (750–550 B.C.), which represented the work of a series of poets, the Greeks observed a primitive religion in which the Olympian gods were represented, and which was tribal rather than personal. One of their earliest myths was that of Gaea and her son Uranus, by whom she had several children who turned out to be monsters, including the one-eyed Cyclops. Uranus was so horrified that he tried to bury them, but his mother grew resentful and arranged for one of their sons, Cronos, to attack and mutilate him when he was retiring to bed with her. His genitals were thrown out to sea and some of the drops of black blood fell on the land and gave birth to the Furies.

Those that fell in the sea produced a fine foam out of which Aphrodite (Venus) was born.

Rites were performed which by sympathetic magic were intended to further the interests of the tribe, particularly those concerned with fertility, whether vegetable, animal or human. These rituals, it is believed, generated great collective excitement, which presumably dispelled the fears of famine by a sense of collective security in which the individuals concerned sank their sense of separateness (equivalent to ontological anxiety) and felt themselves at one with the whole tribe, unfortunately not until a sacred animal or a human being had been ceremonially sacrificed and eaten. No doubt this gave substance to the theme of the one in relationship to the many, of the scapegoat theme, of the one dying that the many might live.

In due course these fertility rites developed into the cult of Dionysus (Bacchus). The *Bacchae* of Euripides describes the rituals, which included the joy of the quick red fountains of wine, and what had originated from a fertility rite developed into a sexual orgy. These rituals included the worship of Pan – perhaps derived from the word Paon, meaning feeder or shepherd, and a goat was sacrificed, as the people were too poor to afford a bull, and it is interesting to note that the word 'panic', which is so often applied to crowds, referred to the mental state produced by the god Pan. The intoxication was considered to be a form of divine madness, and the cult included many barbaric customs, such as the tearing of wild animals to pieces and eating them raw. The result was 'enthusiasm', a word meaning that the god entered the worshipper, and the word 'orgy' originally meant sacrifice. For instance, one of these religious communities (Arcadia), where Hermes and Pan were worshipped, contained a sect of supposed werewolves who practised human sacrifice and cannibalism. It was believed that whoever partook himself became a werewolf and thereafter lost his shadow. At a later day and age Durkheim, Cooley, Mead and Simmel in their own ways were concerned with the problem of social control, and saw the phenomenon of 'internalization' as intimately tied up with the interaction of the individual with others in small groups. Indeed, if there is any preoccupation which has been more characteristic of small group theory than the interest in leadership, it is the more general theme of social control and interest in the social conditions under which the motivation of individuals is most effectively mobilized.

The Greek tragedies grew out of the rites of Dionysus, and the Bacchic respect for violent emotion was once again expressed in the purifying and purging effect of pity and fear (catharsis) provoked by these plays. Euripides describes also the curious element of feminism which developed, in which respectable matrons and maidens would spend entire nights on bare hills in large companies in dances which stimulated ecstasy, both mystical and alcoholic.

The whole cult became spiritualized with the advent of Orphism, a religio-philosophical movement allegedly started by the mythical Orpheus, a priest and philosopher who believed in reincarnation, in the ceremonies of purification including abstinence from animal food except on ritual occasions. Socrates, Pythagoras and Plato were all influenced by this cult. People hoped by practising prudence, foresight, pure living and austerity to influence favourably their destiny after death. They developed an elaborate theology concerning Dionysus, who was reputed to be twice born, once of his mother and reborn again after being torn to pieces by the Titans, from the thigh of his father. In the ritual of devouring the wild animal, symbolizing the eating of Dionysus by the Titans, there was an incarnation of the god in the consumer, who therefore retained a spark of divinity. Socrates was regarded as an Orphic saint; and in the dualism of heavenly soul and earthly body, was believed to have achieved complete mastery of soul over body.

The Orphists developed also a philosophy as distinct from a theology (600 B.C.). They taught a symbolism in which the relationship of the one to the many was clearly enunciated. Somewhat later (500 B.C.) Heraclitus, a mystic philosopher who lived about the same time as Pythagoras, evolved this line of thought in his concept that 'all things came out of the one and the one out of all things; but the many have less reality than the one, which is God', which could have the implication that the individual is less important than the group. He taught that there was a unity in the world, but a unity formed by the combination of opposites, a concept later elaborated by the conflict theory sociologists, for instance Marx.

To recapitulate, in its initial stages, the Hellenic culture was greatly influenced by the introverted Egyptian and extroverted Babylonian civilizations and assimilated from them their magic and fertility rites. These included astrology and a smattering of astronomy and geometry. Out of this, with considerable energy and originality, the Greeks developed along three main directions. First, in their religion, which became the Bacchic and later the Orphic cults. Secondly, in philosophy, they developed a religion-free speculative phase, which marked the enormously significant achievement of the beginning of philosophy round about 600 B.C. Thirdly, in science. Initially, philosophy and scientific speculation had not been treated separately, but in 585 B.C. scientific speculation and hypothesis, less affected by the intrusion of religious, anthropormorphic and ethical considerations, was initiated by the Milesian triad, of whom Thales was the first. He was the initiator of both philosophy and science, which gave rise to the Milesian school and later to the Atomists (430 B.C.) a thorough-going materialistic group for whom the soul was composed of atoms. They considered the world and animals were not created but evolved, and became engaged in a vigorous but disinterested effort to understand the world. They placed less emphasis on man as compared with the universe.

Thereafter the emphasis centred progressively but idealistically more upon men themselves, how we think rather than what we think (the Sophists), the ethics and dialectical method of Socrates (c. 450 B.C.), the religious trends of Plato (c. 400 B.C.), and the anthropomorphism and teleology of Aristotle (c. 350 B.C.). In his *Politics*, Aristotle set forth the importance of the city-state – he recommended that the population should be strictly limited, and saw the political community as the principal source and sustainer of typically human life. It is interesting that he criticized Plato's Utopia on the grounds that it gave too much unity to the state and would turn it into an individual.

The magico-religious theme evolved through the cult of Bacchus, which was itself derived originally from Egyptian and Babylonian fertility cults, and through them to the Orphic rites which were religio-philosophical and profoundly influenced Socrates, Plato and Aristotle. They in their turn passed on a great tradition to the Christians and Scholastics – for instance St Augustine was influenced by Plato and St Thomas Aquinas by Aristotle. The theology of the Church was Greek, its history Jewish and its canon law Roman. St John and the early Christians identified

Christ with the Greek spiritual intellectual principle of *logos*, 'cosmic reason'. This gives intelligibility and order to the world, to words, to things a bridge between the one and the many, the principle that brings back the one to the many and man back to God. Thus it is the Saviour of the world; with nature it orders, with fate it regulates and with providence it guides. God made cosmos out of chaos via logos. Unlike the Jewish and Christian God, the Greek God did not create the world out of nothing, but rearranged pre-existing material out of chaos. The particular characteristic spirit of a community, also its moral purpose, was designated 'ethos'. The Neoplatonists (Plotinus 205–270 B.C.) had already worked out a triad of the One, of the Spirit (logos), and of the Soul, which were to form the metaphysical background to the Holy Trinity.

Socrates is claimed to have said (for he never committed himself to writing) that virtue was knowledge and knowledge was true when it could be defined. He taught heuristically with the aid of the group setting, imparting no information, as he claimed to have none. He asked pivotal questions, and evolved the theory of 'anamnesis', as it was called, whereby he used a method based on the belief that children are born with knowledge already in their souls, which they cannot recall without some outside help (reminiscent of Carl Rogers's client-centred therapy).

Socrates' pupil Plato taught Aristotle, who instructed 'peripatetically', that is whilst strolling up and down a covered pathway in the Lyceum, which necessarily could only have been possible in small groups. It was Aristotle who proclaimed man to be a *zoon politicon*, a social animal, and who, in appreciating the relevance of the individual in relationship to social cohesion, commented that a person 'who is unable to live in society or who has no need because he is sufficient to himself must be either beast or a God'. Russell wrote (1946) that the ethical and aesthetic bias of Plato did much to kill science. Philosophy, as distinct from theology, began in Greece in the sixth century B.C. After running its course in antiquity it was again submerged by theology as Christianity rose and Rome fell. Its second greatest period, from the eleventh to the fourteenth century A.D. was dominated by the Catholic Church.

The third period from the seventeenth century to the present day is dominated more than either of its predecessors by natural philosophy as it was formerly called or science. In fact Socrates, Plato and Aristotle were primarily concerned with human values and with the human situation. They were the predecessors of the social scientist, and the outstripping of political science by nuclear physics, looked at from their viewpoint, would seem to have justified their concern. Socrates, with the help of the voice of his *daimon*, tried to convert philosophy from a study of nature generally to the study of man in particular, of man's soul, a concept which was endorsed not only because of theological learning, but because it drew attention to the essential inner coherence, unity and purposiveness believed to prevail in mental life. 'God orders me to fulfil the philosopher's mission of searching into myself and other men,' he said, 'I have nothing to do with physical speculations', thereby deflecting the drift of contemporaneous philosophy towards a concern with human happiness and futurity. Human beings had three aspects, a body, a psyche (or mind) and a spirit or soul. For him, virtue was knowledge which proceeded from the soul. His view of the soul, in contrast to that of the Christian ethic, was that it was inherently virtuous and had only to be discovered through the precept 'know thyself' (reminiscent of the later concepts of *Dasein* and *Pour Soi* of the existentialists and also the process of free association of the psychoanalysts, a process which had to be aided by the outside help of the analyst. Indeed, Socrates is sometimes claimed to be the first of the existentialists).

The atomism of his contemporary Democritus marks the end of the line of pre-Socratic philosophy which had begun with Thales. A hundred and fifty years previously the latter's 'discovery of nature' signalled the break of cosmogony from theology. Now atomism was not a mere scientific hypothesis, but a thorough-going materialistic and completely closed system of philosophy from which the spiritual had simply disappeared. It held that the enduring, impenetrable core of reality consisted of atoms. The soul also consisted of these atoms, only they were spherical in shape and so could move more easily and slip in between the angular and less mobile atoms of the body. A physical event was explained by taking it to pieces, therefore 'analysing' it, which is derived from the Greek word meaning 'to break up', describing it in terms of smaller physical events. Socrates openly declared he was not interested in how things happened, for he felt this was really of little help to us as human beings, and left us none the wiser. He was only interested in the question of why. He was interested in human affairs, in human relationships, in the relationships of the one to the many in society, and it was over this split between himself, Socrates, the individual and the State of Athens that, because he felt he could not be accepted, because the individual could not be accepted honestly by the social structure of the state, for him at any rate existence or life was no longer worth living. Therefore he made no attempt to escape the sentence of death, which he could so easily have done for a small sum of money, a small fine.

It is possible, therefore, to classify the development of early Greek philosophy into four phases:

(1) The complete and universal materialism of the atomists, such as Democritus, a contemporary of Socrates.

(2) The turning away from this by Socrates from external events towards a concern with the inner world of the individual in relationship to society.

(3) The discovery by Plato of the universal mathematical concepts of Pythagoras which led him to conceive of a universal soul which imposed ideal forms upon matter and nature, and therefore made it more tolerable to relate once again with nature, which Socrates had repudiated.

(4) The attempt by Aristotle to integrate the ideal forms with matter primarily in the biological field and in his study of motion, which represented the first attempt at empirical, inductive, as distinct from deductive reasoning. The balance of philosophical thinking, therefore, remains weighted on the side of speculation and deductive reasoning. On the part of Socrates, with his clear sense of what could and could not be known, this was quite explicitly tied up with his concern with the 'why' of the inner world and the self, and with an indifference towards the 'how' of empirical knowledge as being insufficiently evolved to be taken seriously, but still to be basically questioned.

In principle, the split that existed between the atomism of Democritus and the humanism of Socrates exists in equivalent terms today in an immense array of dualistic shibboleths, such as of the one and the many, of the particular and general, the part and the whole of the humanities and science, experience and behaviour, existence and essence, of rationalism and empiricism, subject and object, of reason versus causes, of mind and body, of *Pour Soi* and *En Soi*, of interpretation and explanation, of noumena and phenomena, of solipsistic and consensual, of fantasy and fact, of 'inner' and 'outer' worlds, of unconscious and conscious, of macrocosm and microcosm, of psychology and sociology, of philosophy and science, of individual and group, of the Idea of Plato versus both the poetry of the gods and the physics of Aristotle of *credo ut intelligam* versus *cogito ergo sum*, of applied and pure science, etc., an endless list of dichotomies.

The Anglo-American philosopher Whitehead who deplored this 'bifurcation of knowledge' remarked that 'twenty-five hundred years of Western philosophy is but a series of footnotes to Plato'. Only relatively recently has the main attention been focused on the nature of this dichotomy itself, as to whether this is relative or absolute; on relationship and communication, for instance in social philosophy, in the dialectical materialism of Marxism, involving the relationship of the antinomies of thesis, antithesis and synthesis; in philosophy, in phenomenology in which the subject intends the object, in sociological phenomenology where the emphasis is on the intersubjective, the inter-experience and the inter-human. For Heidegger it is Dasein, the being-in-the-situation who is regarded as the central unit for study; in logical positivism, for example Carnap, in advancing the theory that all philosophical problems are synthetical, and that when errors in syntax, that is in arrangement or relationship, are avoided, a philosophical problem is thereby either solved or shown to be insoluble.

In psychology, gestalt theory's primary focus is on the relationship of the part to the whole, and in physics quantum theory has drawn our attention to the relationship of the observed to the observer, and to the fact that such things as 'waves' are mental constructs, that the division between subject and object is not absolute but relative, and must be viewed as a single unit if any precision is to be achieved. In psychoanalysis the transference – counter-transference relationship has become the cornerstone of the therapeutic process and the emphasis is now not on explaining causes, but on the semantic one of making sense and giving meaning. Finally in small-group psychotherapy the relationships and the intercommunications between individuals in a social situation, the group matrix, has come to be regarded by many workers as of paramount significance.

To recapitulate, in broadest terms the religious phase gave way to the philosophical with the Milesian school, whose systematic speculation of a scientific nature covered the sixth century B.C. The next step began about the fifteenth century, when deductive logic gave precedence to inductive logic with the rise of the empirically determined applied science of Copernicus, Kepler, Galileo and Newton. Descartes, the founder of modern philosophy, Bacon, Hobbes, Locke, Berkeley, and Hume all participated in rendering philosophy more compatible with the developing physical sciences. This phase has been characterized as the first scientific revolution.

The third step began during the nineteenth century with the increasing concern for communication and overall social relationship. Comte, in reflecting the spirit of his age, rose against the tendency to propound philosophical doctrines without regard to the facts of society, and Marx propounded a whole social philosophy based on contemporary scientific and industrial developments, on history and social institutions, and on mankind not just in relationship to himself, but in relationship to history, to materialistic development and to the community as a whole.

The fourth stage beginning with Kierkegaard (1813–1855) represents an increasing emphasis on the forgotten inner world of the individual in relationship to God and society not in isolation nor destroyed by the technology of modern industrialization, but in valid communication. Above all it represents an attack on all dualisms including that of the individual in relationship to the modern industrial community. The phenomenologists, the ontologists and the existentialists represent this school, and pre-dated in philosophy what later became widely applied in sociology and psychology in general, and group psychotherapy in particular.

Transposing this whole philosophical outlook to the present situation in psychiatry, what strikes one is not the essential gap between causal and semantic theory, but their essential relatedness,

essential also if humanity is to survive. If we omit to trans-
late the meaning of causes, or instead continue to consider meaning
as causally irrelevant, to regard experience and meaning as unscientific and to take them out of the syntax of the scientific orbit,
to regard science as divorced from meaning, the outcome may well
prove disastrous for humanity as a whole.

Turning our attention to the more immediate perspective of
contemporary psychology in relationship to philosophy, we find
concern echoed in the work of many writers. For instance, Gordon
Allport remarks that the greatest failing of the psychologist at the
present time is the inability to prove what he knows to be true. This
has resulted in psychology considering itself to be bullied by the
instruments of physics, to the neglect of that most sensitive of all
recording instruments, namely the human mind itself. 'Heaven
help the psychologist nowadays who doesn't know his computers
and electrical circuits.' 'In earlier days every major philosopher
was also a psychologist' or had been scientifically trained in some
branch of the sciences of the day. Clearly in the move initiated by
Husserl, and continued by Heidegger and also in the psychiatry of
William James, Karl Jaspers, Rollo May and Laing, this valued
intercommunication remains very much alive, particularly for
psychotherapy. The reason is partly circumstantial. The therapist
has to go beyond what can be scientifically validated in the forms of
science as we know them today, for the simple reason that he deals
with the becoming, the emergent, the unique, the individual with
peculiarities, the deviant. He has to work essentially with an
optimistic bias, even if he adopts a stance of provocative nihilism
or non-involvement. Partly in the very nature of his discipline he is
involved with interpretations as well as description, inference as
well as observation, with actual knowing as distinct from knowing
about, with empathy and identification as the primary source of
cognition, as well as observation, of understanding the simple
reductionist elements only in terms of the more complex, for while
conventional science assumes we explain the more complex by the
more simple, the meaning of the more simple can only be understood and interpreted in the framework of the more complex.

George Kelly, in his book *The Psychology of Personal Constructs*
(1955), writes that American psychology has recently turned much
of its attention to the problems of theory building. There has

been a revival of interest in philosophy, particularly in the philosophy of science. Just as philosophers began to look around to see what various kinds of thinking men are actually doing, so psychologists have begun to look around to see what kinds of theories scientists in other realms have actually been producing. This is new. To be sure, psychologists used to look to the methodology and content of physiology as ground upon which to build their own new structure. Then physiology was accepted because its facts were presumed to be real, and its methods appeared to be validated by the palpability of its facts, but now psychologists have begun to compare and contrast theoretical structures which characterize the variety of other disciplines. From this examination of what is going on elsewhere arose some of their hope of discovering a better theoretical model for psychology.

In much the same vein Needleman, in the introduction to his translation of the collected papers of Binswanger, states that it would seem then that the only possibility for psychology to exist as a natural science is in the form of behaviourism where, in fact, consciousness has been excluded from the field of enquiry. In behaviourism the dictates of natural science are fully adhered to. What the behaviourist explores are entities that are corporeal, in which the perceiver is eliminated. In short, the subject-matter of behaviourism is one in which the self is excluded from the world it investigates. This is perhaps scientific method, but he asks: 'Is this psychology?' He goes on:

'If the self is excluded, if consciousness is labelled meaningless, if all that we experience as subjective is not only *not* explained, but rendered out of the field of enquiry, we have no longer a science of the self, no longer a psychology but a set of theories about human behaviour that in principle can be verified only by avoiding the very source of verification, the conscious subject himself.'

Carrying through the same line of thought, Rollo May in 1961 wrote:

'The tentative hypothesis, I suggest, is that my being, which by definition must have unity if it is to survive as a being, has three aspects which we may term 'self', 'person' and 'ego'. The 'self' I use as the subjective centre, the experiencing of the fact that I am the one who behaves in thus and thus ways; the 'person' we may take as the aspect in which I am accepted by others, the 'persona' of Jung, the social roles of William James, and the 'ego' we may take as Freud originally enunciated it, the specific organ of perception by which the self sees and relates to the outside world.'

Is psychotherapy a science? Is it an art? Is it a religion, or is it a philosophy? Rollo May, as we have heard, remarks that every form of psychology or psychiatry rests upon some kind of philosophical presupposition. The only error is not to be aware of these assumptions; the only illusion is to deny them. Existential psychology consists precisely of an attack on this dichotomy. First came Husserl's phenomenology, second Heidegger's remarkable book *Being and Time*. The existential view was close to that of the physicists, Bohr and Heisenberg, who insisted that the Copernican separation of subjective man from objective was an illusion.

James Home, in his article 'The Concept of Mind' (1966) stated that the stimulus to write it came from attending scientific meetings at the Institute of Psychoanalysis for ten years. From the first, he was struck by the essential incomprehensibility of the clinical papers, couched in what he had heard called 'technical language', and by what seemed to him to be the philosophical naïvety of the theoretical papers. He goes on to point out that psychoanalysis began as a study of neurosis, and as a hypothesis about neurosis: it may have made little enough stir in spite of its delineation of an etiology linking neurosis with sexual frustration, had Freud not invoked a totally new principle of explanation. This principle of explanation, which ran counter to the tenor of thought prevalent in medicine at the time, and which eventually led him on to formulate his revolutionary ideas about the unconscious mind, was that the symptom could have meaning. That the symptom has meaning, is Freud's basic discovery, a basic insight which opened up the way to an understanding of functional illness and the principles of psychoanalytic treatment.

It is not surprising that in the excitement of so great a discovery and one that opened up such vast new territories Freud should have overlooked the logical implications and theory of the step he had taken. Those implications, are however, very great, for in the mechanistic medicine of Freud's time, as in all organic medicine of our own day, the symptom is logically regarded as a fact, and a fact is regarded as the product of causes. In this, medicine simply follows the practice of chemico-physical science and the canons of thought which were exemplified with special clarity in classical physics. In discovering that the symptom had meaning and basing his treatment on this hypothesis, Freud took the psychoanalytic study of neurosis out of the world of natural science and into the world of the humanities, because a meaning is not a product of causes but the creation of a subject.

Charles Rycroft, in his essay 'Causes and Meaning' (in *Psychoanalysis Observed* 1966) elaborates on the theme of causal and semantic theory which is rampant in psychology today. He points out that psychoanalysis can be differentiated from the organic school of psychiatry and behaviourism (learning theory) by the fact that they regard subjective experiences as a central object of study and not as an awkward contaminant which has to be either ignored or eliminated. He refers to the significance of social factors when he remarks on the variety of the types of patient whose symptoms vanish as they become aware of unconscious and infantile determinants – and that this only occurs if their personalities are basically healthy and are not called into question by either the patients or the analyst. So often, however, symptoms are not solely an individual matter, but involve a social nexus of relations, including the whole personality with fully conscious social values and motives. This raises the question as to where conscious motives can be regarded as causal. He finds no difficulty in seeing unconscious wishes, motives and causes as synonymous, but this becomes much more difficult when applied to conscious phenomena, for once any mental process or group of ideas becomes conscious it becomes part of the whole complex of thoughts, feelings, social values and aspirations which constitute the personality. One of the characteristic functionalized activities of the personality is making decisions (to that extent unpredictable): otherwise one would have to agree that decision is an illusion and that consciousness has no function, which is unlikely.

When Freud propounded his principle of psychic determinism, his aim was to establish a 'scientific psychology', and he hoped to be able to do so by applying to psychology the same principles of causality as were in his time considered valid in physics and chemistry, and as a result of which all vitalistic biological theories were rejected. Freud's grand design was to adopt the same attitude towards the working of the mind, and he believed that his discovery of unconscious mental forces made this project attainable. If, he argued, all mental activity is the result of unconscious mental forces which are instinctual, biological and physical in origin, then human psychology could be formulated in terms of the interacting of forces which were in principle quantifiable, without recourse to any vital mental integrating agency, thus psychology would become a natural science like physics.

However, the principle of psychic determinism remains an assumption, and Rycroft points out that predictability is lacking; that matters of choice are not arbitrary, but are characteristic manifestations of personality and that Freud, though not able to explain the patient's choice causally, was able to understand its meaning, and that the procedure he engaged in was not the scientific one of elucidating causes but the semantic one of making sense of it.

Recognition of the semantic nature of psychoanalytic theory would also undercut the Eysenck-psychoanalysis controversy and the tendency of analysts to engage in futile argument as to whether the cause of neurosis is to be found in the first three months or years of life, or whether the fundamental cause is constitutional envy of the mother's breast, or is to be found in the oedipal phase of childhood, or in the infant's sensitivity to environmental impingements. It would free them to concentrate on improving their technique for getting into communication with those who have become alienated for whatever causes.

Rycroft points out that one type of neurosis does in fact have a cause – the traumatic neurosis – but this does not fit into psychoanalytic theory, as Freud regretted: 'their relations to determinants in childhood have hitherto eluded investigation'. 'Perhaps the principle of psychic determinism applies to the "false self" while the "true self" has free will.' He ends up by invoking communication again: '. . . psychoanalysis could be regarded as a semantic bridge between science and biology on the one hand and religion and the humanities on the other,' and psychoanalysis's metaphysical status might be 'something *sui generis* which could not be fitted into any of the traditional categories'. He quotes David Cooper's remark that 'Human reality is that section of reality where totalization is the very mode of being', and also Sartre's remark from *Being and Nothingness* to the effect that, until one establishes one's self as the centre of one's own world instead of being an object for someone else, one remains as shameful object, draining away 'my world' into the world of the other.

In another essay in the same book, 'Psychoanalysis – Freudian or Existential?' Peter Lomas makes the point that, despite Freud's basic insight and discovery that the symptom has meaning (referred to in Home's paper), the existentialists have a tendency to discredit Freud as reductionist and dehumanizing. He feels that there is a pressing need for a radical reformation of psychoanalysis, since Freud had had to transcend the language difficulties of the mechanistic terminology of medicine and science of his day and age. He sees a link between the existential concept of alienation and Freud's construct of repression. He states: 'Psychotherapy constitutes the only real challenge and alternative to the barren, organic school of psychiatry that holds sway in this country and its practitioners cannot afford to be catastrophically divided among themselves. It would be a great pity if the "Freudian" and the "existential" schools of thought grew apart rather than together.'

Even though the ego psychology of Hartmann and the work on identity by such writers as Erikson have attempted to extend the importance of the ego in Freud's theory of instinctual drives and structural model of id, ego and super-ego, it has taken the vigour of such existentialist writers as Heidegger, Sartre, Binswanger, Straus, Rollo May and Laing (who, although a trained psycho-analyst, acknowledges his 'main intellectual indebtedness to the existential tradition') to point out that the person cannot be ade-quately formulated in the terminology of natural science. Existen-tial analysis starts without the encumbrance of a system of psycho-logy based on the physical sciences, and views the person as a whole being, the agent of his actions.

Laing stresses the totalizing aspect of the person struggling to maintain his identity in the face of the *total life experience* as opposed to the Freudians' and Kleinians' reduction of matters to instinct theory, to part object relationships which deliberately exclude the present life circumstances of the patient. The differ-ences then centre round time perspectives and the relationship of the part to the whole, reminiscent of the one to the many; for the existential analysts see that the simpler can only be understood in terms of the more complex, a guiding principle which is in opposition to conventional science and the Freudian model, where the more complex is reductively analysed and explained in terms of the more simple, the ampliative or synthetic as Kant described it, as distinct from the merely explicative or analytic.

There has been a tendency, therefore, for Freudian and existential psychoanalysis to grow apart, for whilst the Freudians consider the intrapsychic instinctual 'inner world' as distorted and therefore as inevitably leading to repression and self-alienation, Laing sees the outer world of society as leading to the false shell of a synthetic self. In the setting of the small group these two extremes are regarded as part of a continuum which can be totalized rather than as necessarily split or repressed. The word 'authentic' is derived from a Greek word meaning self-sufficient as distinct from the Aristotelian notion that a person who is unable to live in society is either a beast or a god. The essence of the inconsistency would seem to rest with the question of communicability, as to whether the self feels sufficient security with others to communicate and share. In this lies the crux of the matter, for no one is 'authentic' in isolation any more than a group can be 'authentic' except in relation to the individuals who constitute the group.

The essence of small group psychotherapy lies in the treatment of the individual in a social context where group alienation and self-alienation are revealed simultaneously and operationally in mutual interplay as a unit for study; where for instance, character disorders are manifested as self-evident, pseudo-social adjustments, which is why it is so difficult to treat their distortions in the analytic setting, since the analyst has then to act as an intermediary with social reality. I imagine that alienation more aptly refers to the outer world of the self, that self-alienation refers to the outer world of other people, and repression to the inner world of the self and that self-alienation refers to two selves, one authentic and the other not, and can never therefore refer to the total person.

Philosophy reserves the right to exist if only as a watchdog of scientific method and of philosophy itself, with the result that today there are two principal outlooks. One questions the adequacy of philosophy in relation to science and has virtually voted itself out of court, namely logical positivism. The other does the reverse, and questions the adequacy of science in relation to philosophy – in particular to psychology – namely phenomenology and existentialism.

Logical positivism, representing the outlook which questions the adequacy of philosophy in relation to science, was founded by a small group of philosophers in 1924 known as the Vienna circle, In due course it extended to a wider movement influenced from four main sources: (i) from the older empiricists, for instance Hume and Mill; (ii) from the methodology of empirical science, for instance quantum physics and relativity (Planck, Bohr, Heisenberg and Einstein); (iii) from mathematics and the logical analysis of language, for example Frege, Whitehead and Russell, Wittgenstein, Carnap, etc.; (iv) from the type of psychology of the behaviourists (Pavlov, Watson, etc.). Their basic tenet is to question the validity, as we have said, of philosophy in relation to science and to look for a united science, with a reconstruction and integration of the sciences, this being philosophy's main function, guided by the two basic enquiries of 'What do you mean?' and 'How do you know?' Neither a world view nor a way of living is the primary aim, which is in contrast to theology and metaphysics. These it regards as offering solutions to 'pseudo-problems' arising out of linguistic confusion, since philosophy itself has, as yet, no agreed or precise terminology.

The systematic pursuit of the problem of meaning by means of the logical analysis of language distinguishes logical positivism from the earlier types of empiricism, positivism and pragmatism. Semantic analysis and syntax are studied, the language about language, the meta-language, the hierarchy of language, the relationship of words to words rather than the words themselves. The essence of this 'new' philosophy, as Russell calls it, is to abandon the claim to a special philosophical method or a peculiar brand of knowledge to be obtained by its means, and regards philosophy as essentially one with science, differing from the special sciences merely by the generality of its problems and by the fact that it is concerned with the formation of hypothesis where empirical evidence is still lacking.

Physics and psychology then, have approached each other and the old dualism of mind and matter has broken down. Russell puts it that this modern philosophy of pluralism and realism has, in some ways, less to offer than earlier philosophy. In the Middle Ages philosophy was the handmaid of theology and to this very day, they continue to come under the same heading in booksellers' catalogues. It has been generally regarded as the business of philosophy to prove the great truths of religion. The new realism does not profess to be able to prove them or even to disprove them. It aims only at clarifying the fundamental ideas of the sciences and synthesizing the different sciences in a single comprehensive view over that fragment of the world that sciences have succeeded in exploring. It does not know what lies beyond. It possesses no talisman for transforming ignorance into knowledge; it offers intellectual delights to those who value them, for it does not attempt to flatter human conceit as most philosophers do. It is dry and technical, it lays the blame on the universe which has chosen to work in a mathematical way, rather than as poets or mystics might have desired. Perhaps this is regrettable, Russell says, but a mathematician can hardly be expected to regret it. In this, Russell clearly states that philosophy has changed its Scholastic role of being the handmaid of theology to that of being the handmaid of science, but in company with the early Wittgenstein, who said 'whereof one cannot speak, thereof one must be silent,' he concludes that metaphysics is largely meaningless because most of its statements are pseudo-statements which can neither be verified nor falsified empirically or experimentally, nor can it be analysed and proved absurd or contradictory.

This is surely a very constricted definition of the word 'meaningless' – meaningless because it cannot be mathematized. Somewhere along the line, the logical empiricists have succeeded in begging the question, particularly when this technique of questioning is transposed to the realm of psychotherapy, to the problem of the meaning as distinct from the cause of a symptom. For example, Herbert Feigl, one of the founder members of the Vienna circle, in describing logical empiricism, states that logical analysis 'does not subscribe to any school of psychology, although it is in essential agreement with the methodological outlook of behaviourism, (but not necessarily with its scientific results and certainly not with an unqualified rejection of introspective techniques). This is simply a consequence of the acceptance of an inter-subjective criterion of factual meaning for science.' Phrases such as 'factual meaning' and 'cognitive meaning' are confusing in this context of psychiatry, if cause and meaning are being differentiated from each other. However, this is now regarded as a reductive fallacy by the logical empiricists themselves. It appears they not only restrict the meaning of the word 'scientific', but also confuse a pre-scientific attitude (manifesting 'a not fully liberated pre-scientific type of mind') with a pre-scientific subject for study (which is crucial in a pre-scientific subject such as psychotherapy). In fact the hypothetico-deductive attitude towards a pre-scientific subject is inevitable and scientifically respectable.

The non-cognitive meaning of language (with its emotive and appeal function, inspirational, imaginative, volitional, motivational, and directive), is condemned by faint praise as suitable for 'common life', indispensable in the pursuit of practical life, education, propaganda, poetry, literature, religious edification and moral exhortation, but virtually outside the orbit of logical empiricism (and therefore by implication of philosophy generally), whose primary concern is with cognitive informational and scientific meanings, either purely formal, or logico – arithmetical or factual and empirical. Their emphasis on the relational logical significance of syntax however, is central for communication theory, and this more rigorous attitude towards exactitude over terminology carries a salutary message.

Husserl's creation of phenomenology, on the contrary, represented the outlook which questioned the adequacy of science in relation to philosophy, directly defied the trend within nineteenth-century philosophy which tried to imitate the natural sciences. It forestalled claims by contemporary scientists, psychologists in particular, that they were the sole interpreters of man and his world, and Heidegger recalls the very purpose of philosophy itself, namely to question the meaning of the world and of human life, unrestrained by myth or dogma, and to provide answers to questions so marvellously presented in the great systems of thought. Philosophy had shunned its first and vital task of questioning by the person of his own life. Existentialism restored this question to its central position. Phenomenology plays the role in descriptive psychology that logistical philosophy, mathematics, and geometry play in the natural sciences.

There was, therefore, an irreconcilable divergence at the cores of the logical positivist and the phenomenologist orientations. Carnap admits to a sharp dichotomy in the classification of the sciences which is crucial – namely the distinction between the formal 'pure' deductive sciences (logic and mathematics), and the factual inductive 'applied' sciences (natural and social). It is precisely here in this area that psychology lies, between the humanities and science, where man is both object and subject, where both the worldly and the other-worldly, the tough and the tender, the observer and the observed, constitute the subject matter and themselves come under investigation. It is here that phenomenology and existentialism seem to be asking the crucial questions, and it is indicative of a bias that neither phenomenology nor Husserl, nor Kierkegaard receive any mention in Russell's *History of Western Philosophy* (first published 1946).

As we have said, whilst the logical positivists question the adequacy of philosophy in relation to science, phenomenology and existentialism question the adequacy of science in relation to philosophy, reserving the right of philosophy to act as a watchdog of both science and philosophy itself. The logical positivists, on the contrary, consider that a stage has been reached where such a function is really redundant and that we have now a science of science; and metaphysics has been rendered effete by the developments in mathematics, the logical analysis of language and science – a statement incidentally which is itself metaphysical.

In this context it is interesting to hear again Aristotle's definition of metaphysics, for it was he who first created the subject, and psychology to begin with was an aspect of metaphysics and lay in the domain of philosophy, 'moral philosophy' as it was called, a science of the soul possessing an inner coherence. Till ninety years ago, every major psychologist was also a philosopher and vice versa, but with the introduction of experimental physiological psychology as an aspect of biology, it became an empirical science dealing with facts. Aristotle said:

'There is a science that studies being as being, and the attributes that belong to it by virtue of its being itself. This science is different from all those that are said to deal only with a part of being. None of the other sciences make a universal enquiry into being as being; they cut off a bit of being and then study its attributes – the mathematical sciences, for instance, do this. But since we are seeking for the first principles and the ultimate causes, plainly it is of some nature considered just as itself that they must be causes. So if those who looked for the elements of everything that there is were, in fact, looking for these first principles, the elements of being must be elements of it *qua* being, not accidentally. Hence, we too must understand the elements of being as being.'

If the word 'consciousness' were substituted for 'being' in that quotation, I think perhaps one would get an idea of what Husserl aspires to achieve in phenomenology, namely the study of subjective experience of consciousness as such.

Husserl's concluding passage in *Cartesian Meditations* (1929) is also worth quoting in this context: 'The Delphic motto "know thyself" has gained a new significance. Positive science is a science lost in the world. I must lose the world by *epoché* (bracketing it off) in order to regain it by a universal self-examination.' 'Do not wish to go out,' says Augustine, 'go back into yourself. Truth dwells in the inner man.' Heidegger, the pupil of Husserl, who succeeded him in 1929 as professor at Freiburg and who is regarded as a leading phenomenologist and existentialist, remarks:

'We must return to the inner independence of philosophy from the special sciences. Before a start can be made in the radical analysis of human existence, the road has to be cleared of the objections of philosophic tradition – science, logic and common sense. The moderns have lost hard-won insights of man into metaphysical reality only possible through a "destructive" analysis of the traditional philosophies.'

By this recovery of the hidden sources, Heidegger aims to revive the genuine philosophizing which has vanished for us in the Western world because autonomous science seriously disputes the position of philosophy.

Whilst the 'brass instrument', 'motorized' psychology of Wundt, the instinct theory of McDougall, the 'ebullient reflexology' of Watsonian behaviourism, learning theory, behaviour therapy and the organicist trend in psychology are in line with the development of logical empiricism, phenomenology relates to such trends as gestalt psychology, psychoanalysis in certain of its aspects, existential psychiatry, group psychotherapy and psychotherapy generally.

Phenomenology, which on the Continent is regarded as marking the turning-point in twentieth-century philosophy, is extraordinarily difficult to understand in its entirety, possibly owing to the obscurity in which Husserl's writings are couched, and the following account certainly does it no justice. What is phenomenology? Merleau-Ponty, regarded as one of the more technically competent philosophers among the French phenomenologists, asked this in 1962, and remarks that it is strange that the question has still to be asked over half a century after the first works of Husserl were published. The fact remains that it has by no means been answered. Yet it has concurrently given birth to significant developments in both philosophy and psychology, and though Freud gives no acknowledgement of the fact, his description of the *technique* of free association bears a striking resemblance to Husserl's phenomenological approach of experiences reduced and freed of all presuppositions, 'the stream of pure experiences of a single experiencing individual, the stream of cogitationes'. It is perhaps significant that Husserl was the most prominent disciple of Brentano whose lectures Freud attended for two years, and both Husserl's and Freud's *magnum opus* appeared concurrently in the year 1900. Both writers were instrumental in cutting the ties between logic and psychology, a universe of absolute freedom from prejudice.

Husserl himself defined phenomenology as the study of the structure of consciousness, the study of experience, of subjectivity. Thevenaz has described it as the study of the point of contact where being and consciousness meet. Since Descartes and *until* Husserl, consciousness had been taken for granted as a sort of mirror, as so obvious as not to require further elucidation. Philosophy was concerned with man the impersonal abstract knower, confining himself to knowing the external universe and not as in existentialism with a personal, existing, individual human being. For Husserl this left academic philosophy as half a science, as a half-measure, since consciousness is itself prejudiced and distorted; it is not a mirror reflecting the external world accurately; it is not a passive observer. This was confirmed later by Einstein, Planck and Heisenberg who regarded the concept of the passive observer as a fallacy. Neither philosophy nor science can be regarded as securely grounded until we know more about the apparatus of consciousness.

Originally 'phaenomena' meant appearances fundamental to all empirical (experienced) knowledge. Later it became a branch of mental science which Hegel (1807) and Lazarus (1857) differentiated from psychology; the former described phenomena of mental life, the latter sought their causal and genetic explanation. The first to characterize his approach to philosophy as phenomenological was Hegel. However, in whatever context the term phenomenology is used, it refers back to the distinction introduced by Kant between the 'phenomenon' or appearance of reality in consciousness, and the 'noumenon' or being of reality in itself. Kant himself did not develop a phenomenology as such, but since his *Critique of Pure Reason* recognizes scientific knowledge only of phenomena and not at all of noumena, his critique can be considered a sort of phenomenology. Whatever is known is phenomenon, 'appearing' to consciousness, but it is possible to think what is not known, and this we think of as a 'thing-in-itself' or noumenon, of which the phenomen is the known aspect. Kant rejected both the metaphysical emphasis in Hegelianism, which posited that there was no need of even thinking of an unknown thing-in-itself. He rejected the rationalization of Descartes, and also the phenomenism of Hume which based its radical empiricism, the reconstruction of our knowledge of the world, purely on the certainty of direct *sense* experience of sense data.

Husserl (1859–1938), who described his transcendental phenomenology as neo-Cartesian, since it was Descartes who first turned philosophy towards the subject himself, an entirely new kind of philosophy, was the first to apply the name 'phenomenology' to a *whole* philosophy (1900), and when the term 'phenomenology' is used today it usually refers to the philosophy of Edmund Husserl or his followers. He was opposed to what he called the 'dualism' of Kant, the 'constructionism' of Hegel, the 'psychologism' or 'naturalism' of the positivists. In his phenomenological psychology, Husserl was also the first philosopher who focused on personal relationships and the descriptive analysis of subjective processes seen as a special sort of vital experience which he called *Erlebnis*, marking a triumph for subjectivity as such. This is in contrast to the positivism of Ernest Mach and the Vienna circle, who were phenomenological to the extent that they were satisfied with the pure description of consciousness and saw no grounds for becoming involved with affirming a reality, for example, the 'thing in itself' of Kant, a thorough-going non-metaphysical approach which gives the appearance of being so exclusively descriptive as to eliminate reality as an *involvement* altogether, which in its negative way is just as metaphysical as its opposite.

Clearly, phenomenology holds a special appeal for psychotherapists, who so often appear to work 'phenomenologically', whether acknowledged as such or not.

Mind–body relationships have been viewed both monistically, the mind being regarded as a bodily function (so regarded by Aristotle, Hobbes, Hume, Hegel, the behaviourists and logical positivists and presumably the organicists in psychiatry) – and dualistically as one aspect of a two-sided interaction or a two-directional causal relationship (so considered by Plato, Descartes, Lotze, Kant and William James). Others have regarded the relationship of the two as parallel to each other (the Geulincx clocks hypothesis) or as an epiphenomen or by-product. However, even though Descartes pointed out that we cannot be certain of anything except our own consciousness and that therefore philosophy should begin with the study of consciousness, this was in fact the very thing he neglected to do.

It was Husserl, some 260 years later, who pointed out this omission. He considered Descarte's *cogito*, or consciousness to be more than a camera or mirror reflecting reality, and that it was itself worthy of investigation. In fact, as has since been proven experimentally, the camera does lie. What happens if you put a mirror opposite a mirror? No one knows. With people, on the other hand, interaction occurs; to put it modestly, what Brentano and later Husserl called 'intentionality or meaning'. Consciousness aimed and shot at reality, moulding it according to its own structure. Until we have studied the phenomena of its own structure, until we understand the distortions it imposes on reality as reflected in human consciousness, we shall never succeed in interpreting reality scientifically. Husserl took the obvious step which has eluded philosophers for over two centuries, of suggesting that we inspect the mechanics of the instrument, that is, of consciousness itself, and suggested we make a distinction between the appearance and the thing which appears. In brief, Descartes pointed out that the objects on the mirror of consciousness are not the objects themselves, and Husserl suggested we look at the mirror itself.

Husserl, however, unlike Descartes and Kant, was not a dualist. His world was one of 'pure' phenomenology. Kant's world of fact, of things-in-themselves (noumena), is for Husserl not another world but simply *is not*. It simply does not exist as a separate entity. He considered that Descartes, in discovering the transcendental ego, was on the brink of an infinite realm of being of a new kind, a new idea of the grounding of knowledge, that he stood on the threshold of the greatest of all discoveries and that Descartes, in not going far enough, never really grasped the full significance of his discovery and did not pass through the gateway that leads into a genuine transcendental philosophy.

Descartes, like his contemporary in England, Francis Bacon, felt the importance of making a clean sweep of countless universal assumptions obstructing the progress of knowledge. What Husserl attempted to do was to carry this through. Not content with investigating the world, he asks us to focus our attention on the ego itself, to sweep aside these countless universal assumptions and prejudices we have developed in causal psychology, and try and describe pure consciousness itself, the formal structure of the phenomenal world, freed from interpretations, evaluations, causal and genetic and often spurious explanations. After this reduction, as he called it, what is left is a stream of pure experience, of a single experiencing being, my own perceivings, rememberings and imaginings. The world has become a bracketed world, it is merely a phenomenon for my transcendentally reduced consciousness. Essentially it means a state of pure reflection, and for this the phenomenological nature as a well-defined, unbiased attitude for which all mundane beliefs are not merely suspended temporarily, but for always, as a matter of principle, as long as we wish to work phenomenologically so to speak, is fundamentally different from the 'natural' attitude.

In other words, similar to the process of free-association, Husserl created a system that, as distinct from logical positivism, directs its attention to the internal world, and in so doing directs its attention towards what might be called an empirical subject-ivism 'the detective *is* the murderer', a new attitude to empiricism which approaches subjective experience, complete subjectivity with complete objectivity, that is purely descriptive without prejudice, evaluation or interpretation into other terms, 'the stream of cogitations', all mundane beliefs suspended for always as a matter of principle.

We must all have had the experience of seeking to make a state-ment and of our statement being met by a storm of premature misconceptions, without our being given the opportunity or time ever to complete our sentence. Phenomenology seeks to create an attitude, and approach, a method towards subjectivity as such which gives it a complete, unprejudiced hearing. It is a vast reorientation, and for the first time since Socrates, but on this occasion with the experience of all the intervening two thousand years at our dis-posal, the inner world has become open to systematic investigation in its own terms, being permitted the emergence of its own particular qualities. Up till then either in the form of Descartes' pure reflecting mirror of the mind, the omniscient *cogito*, of the clean slate, the *tabula rasa* of Locke, upon which were thrown the reflections of experienced objects, the mirror and the slate and the mind, the soul or ego, had all been assiduously avoided in their own right, avoided, that is phenomonologically speaking. That the mirror might have its own particular distortions and qualities had pre-sumably been such an offensive and humiliating realization that it had always been denied or disguised behind a smokescreen of protest which took the form of premature evaluations related, no doubt, to a distorted orientation towards subjectivity rather than an 'objective' one.

Nowadays, in general psychological parlance, an unprejudiced attitude has become referred to as phenomenological or as des-criptive, as distinct from genetic psychology. We *ourselves* cannot be bound by the positive orientation of psychological or natural science, for we have no part at all of the objective world, but only by conscious subjective life itself, wherein the world and all its contents are made for us. Once we have 'seen' phenomena, it seems we already have a phenomenology with its own particular principles and glossary of terms. In doing this, not only is psycho-logy and therefore natural science itself, being correctly grounded on a secure foundation of immediate experience, but also the whole of philosophy with its metaphysical problems is being established in a proper perspective for the first time in history. Phenomenology therefore claims to be the culmination of both rationalism and empiricism.

Both consciousness and perception are active processes, moulding and distorting the world and not just passively reflecting it. This, quite apart from emotion, so that consciousness, perception, physical sensation and desire as well as emotion all distort or, as Husserl puts it, 'intend' the world. Examples of intentionality are seeing faces in the clouds, the Rorschach and other projective tests. As already mentioned, consciousness does not merely passively see the world, but fires attention at it, as one might fire a rifle at a target. 'Listening', for instance is not simply a passive process. In 'listening' we make others talk and even say the things we want to hear. We 'read' the world around us; out of the confused mass of sights and sounds we filter off automatically intentionally almost all that do not immediately concern us. We do not even notice them, since intentionality is the fundamental character of subjective processes.

Husserl then not merely revolutionized philosophy, but the whole attitude towards psychology. He maintained in 1931 that true philosophy should seek its foundations exclusively in man's subjectivity; not psychologically, but as a transcendental subjectivity, without which psychology and the other sciences cannot be grounded philosophically. As long as philosophy and psychology confine themselves to the universe and to psychology as a positive science, they will remain only half sciences. The trend of philosophy to proceed in the direction of positive science only has kept philosophy at a standstill for over two hundred and fifty years. It was Husserl who pointed out this simple mistake. He states that it is well known that science, as we Europeans understand it, was created in general and outlined by the Greeks; its original name is philosophy; its object is the universe and whatever exists. It branches out into the social disciplines, whose main branches are called sciences, while only those disciplines are called philosophical which treat questions that apply equally to all that exists. The ancient concept of philosophy as a totality of all the sciences still remains, and will always remain, indispensable.

So we have two stages in philosophical development. First the naïve objectivistic, strictly verifiable, positive, rational science of the pre-Cartesian era, and now the phenomenology of the post-Cartesian period in which Husserl has attempted to raise psychology to a higher scientific level. In the same way that the formal mathematical sciences constitute the great logical instruments for corresponding sciences of facts, where the science of facts, of nature, has only become possible through the independent elaboration of a 'pure' mathematics of nature in which the science of pure possibilities and surmise precedes the science of facts, so phenomenology attempts a science of 'pure' subjectivity. Geometry abstracts from external objects; phenomenology from the experience of the internal equivalents of external objects. Husserl began as a mathematician and had studied pure logic as a theoretical science independent of empirical knowledge. He then decided that a phenomenological analysis was needed to test our metaphysical concepts.

As we shall see, the phenomenological approach was adopted by the gestalt psychologists, and is seen both in the Freudian technique of free association and even more obviously in the process of the free-flowing conversation of group association, in which the configurations of these 'intersubjective' group associations are themselves the subject matter of investigation in the Foulkesian approach, particularly in the specific group feature of locating the foreground figures against the background of the group context. The group analytic psychotherapy setting is one in which the group is given minimal guidance as to direction or content, and in which the usual features evident in other groups formations, such as clear task, leadership and outside contact are, to use Husserl's word, *epochés*, or bracketed off, allowing for the full emergence of a minimally prejudiced or distorted group matrix, namely for the appearing of a group phenomenology.

To summarize, phenomenology is the descriptive study of experience, of the subjective (but not the subject) and of the subjective intended objective, freed as far as possible from interpretation, evaluation, prejudice, explanations and presuppositions, including logic. It offers a descriptive analysis of subjective process and consciousness in so far as the latter intends objects, that it is conscious of, animates and acts upon them. It involves the progressively achieved awareness of what it means to be conscious, that is, free, the primary world of lived experience, a return to things themselves as experienced, of which science as we know it is a second-order expression. Phenomenology is neither a science of objects nor a science of the subject. It is a science of experience, and consciousness is regarded as an active process. The subject and the object are studied in their correlativity to each other, of 'conscious of', of the *Lebenswelt*, of which there are many kinds, for instance:

(a) the impersonal (pre-personal) public;
(b) the human, and socially structured world of inter-subjectivity, of language and communication;
(c) the more personally structured world of specific cultures, social groups, historical epochs;
(d) and finally there are those incommunicable worlds of private experience which each man possesses as his own.

Husserl was not interested in language as such, in words, but in experienced meaning rather than in talk about experience. The 'phenomenon' manifests itself immediately in consciousness, it precedes any reflection of judgement; the phenomenon is that which gives *itself*, prior to the intermediary of words.

The intentionality of phenomenology is characterized by a new relationship between subjective and objective, between thought and being, whereby these are inseparable, and without which neither consciousness nor the world could be grasped. Therefore, 'reality' in itself as an absolute object becomes absurd, unthinkable. This sort of consciousness is transcendental and not psychological and is concerned with the consciousness of meaning.

The *cogito* of Descartes was a disembodied isolated thing which thinks. Husserl, on the other hand, was concerned with intersubjectivity, where various experiences, my own and other people's, intersect and engage, both in the past and the present.

Some writers (S. Koch) have preferred to call phenomenology experientialism, and for the phenomenologist meaning is central and inescapable, and mental life cannot be explained away by a Newtonian philosophy, no longer trivialized as an epiphenomenal by-product. All this, of course, has enormous implications in the intersubjective situation of psychotherapy, and it is a matter of considerable significance for the psychotherapist that here is a philosophy that recognizes there is an equally large area for study inside man himself as there is in the outer world, instead of priding itself on the avoidance of human relationships.

What then might phenomenology as applied to group therapy entail? Seemingly it would suppose an attitude at least on the part of the conductor which is responsive to the appearance of group events that have not been 'imposed' or artificially induced, in which external interferences are minimal, that is to say 'reduced', bracketed off, or *epochés*, and are a spontaneous free expression coming from the members in interaction with each other (inter-subjectivity). For example, contact outside the group situation is kept to a minimum, over-interpretation, unnecessary interventions, irrelevant directives are avoided. There is an absence of prescribed goal, of agenda, or task or occupation, other than actually to meet and be ready to be actively responsive by listening to contributions, rather than simply being passively 'accepting', or 'permissive'. The attitude is fostered that all contributions are relevant, though we may not always know their meanings. There is no sort of contribution that is given priority, that 'should', 'really' be made, such as personal disclosures, nor is there any topic that cannot be introduced (for instance, the weather, chit-chat, nonsense, humour, play, small-talk, religion). There is no such reference as to what the members are 'really' saying or doing.

Untrammelled by vetoes, processes appear, evolve, explicate, and unfold in emerging patterns seemingly 'unconsciously' to the individuals concerned, processes that are characteristic of the group itself and which would not be evident in any other situation to this extent, processes which have been called by Foulkes 'group specific features', and can be classified under the headings of activation, communication and socialization, inherent in the group which enable the individual participants to discover, by creating and being created by these processes, what a group is that can allow these essentials of consciousness, perception, freedom and responsibility to arrive at their full expression, undistorted spontaneously and meaningfully, 'experientially', in relationship to each other.

The individual discovers the meaning of contact and participation with others, and others discover the group experience so that it appears that the group discovers itself. These are impressions which can only in the first place be experienced. Most group therapists know what the experience is of a group appearing often quite suddenly to have 'gelled' – to have become or to have given the appearance of having become a group, of having begun to establish and shape an intersubjective network of communication (the group matrix) which is freely and spontaneously emerging, but which concerns specifically the actual individual members who constitute this particular group. To quote Foulkes:

'There is the free-floating verbal communication carried to an extreme point, there is the maximum reduction of censorship with regard to the content of contributions and to the expression of personal and interpersonal feelings; there is an attitude of the conductor, who not only actively cultivates and maintains the group atmosphere and the active participation of members but also allows himself to become a transference figure in the psycho-analytic sense and accepts the changing roles which the group assign him. . . .'

Another feature that is primarily evident in relationships is that of intentionality. In many ways it is easier to imagine the mind's eye as passively reflecting inanimate objects such as the proverbial table or chair in mechanical terms, like a camera, but the situation becomes infinitely more complex when one of these human cameras or mirrors reflects another's mirror or camera. Foulkes has compared the group to entering a hall of distorting mirrors. Ezriel has described each group member as attempting to manipulate the others into the patterns of his internal object constellations, thus creating a common group tension as a result of these intentions. No group participant is a passive reflecting mirror – nor does the conductor simply sit passively and accept permissively – no one is a pure reflecting cogito. The conductor introduces prejudices from his experiences of other groups for example from the result of his training from other disciplines, from other 'inter-subjectivities' such as psychoanalysis, group analysis, 'expertise'. The other members are more liable to introduce constellations from their past, for instance their family past, though these do not necessarily have to be referred to by interpretation, but can rely on the evolving phenomenology of the group in its own being to provide sufficient contrast to enable these individual distortions to be shed as inappropriately idiosyncratic.

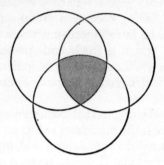

The diagram represents the evolving group matrix between a group of three people which is represented by the shaded area. Each circle represents a subjective area, an 'individual' phenomenological world. Where all three overlap represents the intersubjective area equivalent to a group phenomenology which, as the meetings proceed, will increase in extent and complexity of shapes or metastructures of mutual intentionality in which subjective and intersubjective are essential to and create each other. The private world of a person is his phenomenological world. This may be lacking in essence, may be submerged in the world of, for instance, his father, so that a patient cannot get out of bed in the morning – 'transitivism' as it has been called. He has not yet built up his own boundaries – and it is dangerous to proceed out into the world only to encounter his father's world and be submerged again.

In the group setting, his phenomenological world encounters that of contemporary other subjectivities and a creative process may be set up, with these remoulding and engendering each other – bringing out the essence, the 'purity' of socially more appropriate beings with the shedding of the past – idiosyncratic in this instance – paternalistic world. In the therapeutic group, this encounter with the group phenomena between the absolutely subjective, termed by Husserl the transcendentally reduced ego, and the absolutely subjective of others, appears on occasion to occur in a process of transcendental intersubjective intentionality, a pure essential phenomenological process (alias group therapy) that is, if it be permitted to do so. To quote Husserl (*Cartesian Meditations*, 1929), speaking of objective subjectivity:

'Now however, we are envisaging a science that is, so to speak, absolutely subjective, whose thematic object exists whether or not the world exists'; and, 'Perhaps reduction to the transcendental ego only seems to entail a permanently solipsistic science; whereas the consequential elaboration of this science in accordance with its own sense, leads over to a phenomenology of transcendental inter-subjectivity and, by means of this, to a universal transcendental philosophy.'

Group therapy could be conceived as a form of phenomenology of transcendental intersubjectivity, and the convener of a group has been compared to the conductor of an orchestra, for what could be more phenomenological than music?

In the group situation, from the group viewpoint, as distinct for instance from the psychoanalytic, the subject–object dichotomy simply does not exist, since the subjective of one is concurrently the objective for the other, and it is the transpersonal communicational network, that is the slowly growing group matrix, that goes to constitute what Husserl called the phenomenon of transcendental intersubjectivity.

Society, as Husserl put it (1929) 'which we experience in a common consciousness, may be reduced not only to the individual fields of the individual consciousness but also by the means of an intersubjective reduction, to that which unites these, namely the phenomenological unity of the social life. Thus enlarged, the psychological concept of internal experience reaches its full extent.' The subjective for Husserl therefore has a twofold significance, a double relativity of consciousness with a transcendental and psychological phenomenology, one which relates to the inner world of experience and one which relates to the consciousness of the outer world, the experienced consciousness, the consciousness of or intentionality, and also the intersubjective world of others.

Existentialism further extended the outlook which questioned the adequacy of science in relation to philosophy. Martin Heidegger (1889–1967) is regarded as the leading existentialist writer; pupil and successor to Husserl, he sought, as we quoted, to find a way back to an inner independence of philosophy from the 'special' sciences. He expanded the generalities of Husserl's transcendental subjectivity and consciousness to the specific experience and personal existence of the actual subject. He focused on the actual personal-discrete-being-in-the-world, which he terms Dasein – the actual person there existing in an exact place and at an exact moment in time – an issue which one can choose to sidestep or not, over which one can assume or reject the power of resolute choice. In Heidegger's existential structure of the Dasein the *Da* expressed not so much factual existence, but an area of revealability in which things can manifest themselves as phenomena as distinct from the existential which is the real concrete empirical, given in experience.

At one blow Heidegger destroyed the Cartesian picture of things, bodies, extended substances in contrast to the ego, the immaterial thinking substance of the mind or soul. He characterizes man as essentially a being-in-the-world and his theory of man has been called a field theory of man or of being, analogous to Einstein's field theory of matter. In Kurt Lewin's terms it is much easier to transfer the concept of field theory to a group – to see a group of individuals as a field rather than as individual and to see Heideggers Dasein as being in a group rather than in the world. In choosing to become a being, in creating one's Dasein, Being is also conceived, a valid Human Being in which being can afford to become unhidden and true, as distinct from 'one', the impersonal public creature which it may be less fearful to be than the self, but at the expense of self-evasion. The fearfulness of becoming self may relate not so much to the world, but to an alienating hostile society.

Whilst Husserl unfolded the world from intentional consciousness, Heidegger begins from above. In his later work he postulates Being as a kind of obscure hidden power which opens itself to beings, but it seems less obscure when he suggests that language is centred in Being. 'Even before man thinks and speaks, Being speaks to man and renders language, logic and thought possible.' He was much influenced by Kierkegaard, who considered that truth could not be found in abstract theory or reason (e.g. the 'whole reason' of Luther) but in 'existence'. 'Truth exists only as the individual himself produces it in action.' *Sorge* or concern constitutes the ultimate structure of consciousness and gives rise to *Angst* or dread, and tends to be lost in the distractions and cares of daily life. Its real remedy rests in its confrontation in the light of conscience, of death and in the consciousness of time, and only resolute choice can explain the significance and phenomenon of man's position in daily life and in history. By avoiding concern and Angst, one avoids becoming what one really is, one fails to discover one's Dasein – equivalent to not living, having never faced the nothingness that is there with Dasein. In order to grasp and appreciate the reality of Dasein, one has also to confront the reality of nothingness and death, and to do this one must tolerate Angst – the only alternative is neurotic anxiety, which comes of estrangement from Dasein. So which shall it be, neurotic anxiety or Angst?

For Karl Jaspers authentic existence, or *Existenz*, has a somewhat similar meaning to Dasein. Whilst Kierkegaard saw truth in existence, Husserl saw it as consciousness and pure subjectivity. Heidegger, on the other hand, saw it in the freedom and possibility of the subjective. Jaspers saw it as communicability. These all contain the theme of upholding the one in the face of many – and this has relevance for group therapists in discovering where the therapeutic emphasis lies. For instance Foulkes's final passage in his first book *Group Analytic Psychotherapy* (1948) suggests that a good group 'breeds and develops, creates and cherishes that most precious product – the human individual'.

Jaspers wrote:

'The community of masses of human beings has produced an order of life in regulated channels which connects individuals in a technically functioning organization, but not inwardly from the historicity of their souls. The emptiness caused by dissatisfaction with mere achievement and the helplessness that results when the channels of relation break down have brought forth a loneliness of soul such as never existed before – a loneliness that hides itself and that seeks relief in vain in the erotic or the irrational, whilst it leads eventually to a deep comprehension of the importance of establishing communication between man and man.'

Later he remarked that he was perplexed by people's rigid inaccessibility, since no urge seemed stronger to him than that for communication with others, and that the individual cannot become human by himself; alone, he sinks into gloomy isolation.

It is strange that Jaspers, throughout his massive 900–page tome, *General Psychopathology*, only refers to Husserl in two footnotes, strange insomuch as his line of thought has so much in common with him, ushering in existential analysis by a descriptive phenomenology. 'Phenomenology is for us', he says, 'purely an empirical method of enquiry maintained solely by the fact of patients' communications. It is obvious that in these psychological investigations, descriptive efforts are quite different from those in the natural sciences.' Husserl of course, went further than Jaspers in his later universal philosophy, which supplied an organum for the methodical revision of all the sciences, his transcendental phenomenology or subjectivity as distinct from his earlier phenomenological psychology.

The main differences between phenomenological analysis and existential is that existential analysis operates in a larger framework and does not restrict itself to the investigation of states of consciousness, but takes into account the entire structure of existence of the individual. Phenomenology emphasizes the unity of the individual's inner world, whilst existentialism emphasizes that the individual may live in two or more, sometimes conflicting, worlds.

However, the main break-through for group therapy, whether one is considering Husserl's *Mitwelt*, or Heidegger's *Mitsein*, is the appreciation of the primary significance of intersubjectivity for both phenomenology and existentialism – a Mitsein which allows not only for 'being-with-others' but simultaneously for the owning of 'mineness', for Dasein, the possibility of discovering one's own authentic subjectivity with others, for the opening of communication in what would otherwise be a closed system as, for example, an incommunicable neurotic state.

Heidegger's *Being and Time* reads in places like a very good theoretical commentary on both psychotherapy and group therapy. For instance, he reflects on that aspect of Being-in-the-world which concerns encounter with other people, or *Mitdasein*. Mitsein and Mit-dasein are both essential aspects of Dasein. On the whole, Heidegger uses the narrower everyday meaning of Dasein which stands for the kind of Being that belongs to persons (rather than the more general use for any kind of Being or 'existence' of traditional German philosophy). 'Dasein can only be authentically itself if it makes this possible for itself of its own accord.' 'State-of-mind and understanding are characterized equiprimordially by *discourse.*' 'Dasein is an entity which is in each case I myself; its Being is in each case mine.' At the same time Dasein cannot Be except in the world with others.

Sartre has been greatly influenced by Husserl and Heidegger, and followed up with a similar notion – that of Pour Soi. Man is nothing else but what he makes of himself – that his is the first principle of existentialism; that he strives to escape his Pour Soi (for itself), by retreating into En Soi (in itself). The En Soi signifies all the objects around a man, impermeable, dense, silent, and dead, without meaning; they only are. He denies the old dualisms (even though the Pour Soi and En Soi would still seem to echo them) of body and mind, physical necessity and free will, reality and appearance, as artificial separations of what in reality is whole. He forms a much closer link between man and his world, than Husserl in his interpretation of a subject with a pure consciousness, and he denies Husserl's concept of the transcendental subject altogether. He accepted Heidegger's being-in-the-world but not his Being. However, he is impressed by the concept of intentionality – according to which consciousness is always consciousness of something. The whole world finds no meaning in En Soi, in itself, but only Pour Soi, through itself. Compared to En Soi a person has a strange existence; he has no in-itself, he is a shell which can and must be filled by himself, at each and every moment. To fail to do so is to live inauthentically, in estrangement from what one can be. If one attempts to live as En Soi one encounters nothingness, the opposite of Pour Soi, which instead of being a creative, salutary experience as envisaged by Heidegger, is a shattering warning signal and is accompanied by nausea, boredom, anxiety, forlornness and despair. Sartre's first book (1938) *Nausea* describes just this experience. *Being and Nothingness*, an essay on phenomenological ontology, appeared some twelve years later.

His last philosophical work appeared in 1960, *Critique of Dialectical Reason*, an epic of philosophical, sociological and psychological 'demystification', dealing with sociological and group processes which are described as going through four stages of, first, unorganized seriality, through a primitive grouping stage, to a solidification of organization and finally to the paralysing inertia of institution. Throughout the book he is primarily concerned with matters of freedom, and with individual and collective responsibility.

Wilfred Desan, in *The Marxism of Jean-Paul Sartre* (1966) and R. D. Laing and D. C. Cooper in their book *Reason and Violence* have presented us with a condensation of three of Sartre's most decisive works which includes the *Critique*, as yet untranslated into English. The *Critique* is described as a totalization of the whole of existing socio-historical knowledge. He concludes that the closest place of reality such as we can conceive it, lies in the realm of human history. Sartre is interested in Kant's categories – in particular that of the synthesis of plurality and unity to become a totality, a multiplicity in unity or a unified multiplicity. But as group processes are continuously moving, there are no final totalities in history and some prefer to use the term 'totalization' rather than totality, for though each person's particular point of view is an absolute, it constantly turns out to be relative. This was a process originally conceived of by Hegel, this endless relentless cancellation of one viewpoint by another, and this constitutes his dialectic, which Marx took up in a different form in his dialectical materialism.

Sartre applies the same principle to social totalizations. The fusion of one to a plurality is not a simple addition – the act of perceiving a number of people as *one* constitutes the beginning of a group – one and one make one, a social gestalt or, as Sartre calls it, a totalization, and this he explores phenomenologically. For example, he does not impose family constellation on to a group setting as, for instance, Freud has done; he studies what is actually presented as far as he can 'transitively'. Unless we think dialectically we falsify our perceptions to fit our conceptions, which become reified therefore. As a result, we lapse either into ossified totalistic institutionalism, or alternatively get lost in a forest of hyper-empiricism. Each in its turn should become depassed – whether an individual point of view, a synthesis, or a totalization. Sartre is interested in the properties of certain key totalizations in terms of structure, process, organization, and institutionalization of varying duration.

By way of totalization we constitute ourselves into social collectivities which are real and actual, which we invent, and may attempt
to perpetuate, and to guarantee against detotalization. Often it is
difficult to destroy a group 'being' without destroying the individuals. With group therapists, Sartre asks what the relation is of the
group being to the human beings who comprise it.

Analogical thinking, such concepts as Leviathan, family,
organism, supra-individual, mechanism, etc., have often resulted
in short-circuiting the issue with distortions and artefacts which
such facile ploys tend to generate. It is in these reified collectivities
that so much violation is inflicted on 'human nature' in its fullness –
and there is no escape, since there is no such human being as a
non-group individual. The individual is always riddled by the
particular alienating, socializing, massifying, metamorphosis he
undergoes in being a member of certain particular groups, as
distinct from an imaginary single individual in an unmediated
person-to-person or person-to-world relationship. This is of
course, one of the problems of language, to express in everyday
words, what is not an everyday but personal experience, or
alternatively in scientific terms, for what is mathematized can be
repeated, but no experience can be repeated. To point out the
ambiguities of language (as the organized professional philosophers
of linguistic analysis do) is one thing: the wish to eliminate them is
another, particularly as the human reality in which we live is
fraught with ambiguous fact. All prose is failure. As Laing puts it:
'My experience simultaneously seeks and flinches from its verbal
expression. . . . Language is objectification, it is the occasion of the
other's appropriation of my subjective reality . . . its structure is
always that of being-for-the-other. There is no private interior
language which does not have this structure. The inaudible
utterances of my talking to myself reflect the way I am a quasi-other
to myself.'

Sartre is critical of certain aspects of both American and Marxist
sociology. He regards Kurt Lewin's approach of looking at a group
from outside it as a 'fetishism of totalities'. He regards Gardiner's
concept of 'basic personality structure', produced by the primary
situations of child-rearing of a given culture as mechanistic, and
Marxists as making global judgements, and that American sociology provides an ideological food for the working classes.

Psychoanalysis is for Sartre above all an illumination of the present actions and experiences of a person in terms of the way he has lived his family relationships. In philosophy he sees personal life as 'constituted-constituting'; we mould ourselves out of how we have been moulded, and in his view, psychoanalysis would tend to ignore the active constituting, making, moulding element of personal unity, reducing the person to a resultant heap of instinctual abstractions, which have no place for intentionality in each person's life. His assessment, however, is based on Freud's original metapsychological position and not on the whole range of psychoanalytic writings. He feels that the analyst attempts to make judgements about the analysand from a position of complete exteriority in relation to a biological entity, and that therefore the person disappears. The reductive biologism – the psycho-organistical dualism, the pseudo-irreducibles, end in explaining all but in treating no one, for the relation of self to being cannot be expressed in physicalist metaphor or biological analogizing or in explanations explaining away in a series of mechanisms imposed on a subject objectified in a psychoanalytic framework.

There is, however, plenty of room for a phenomenological examination of 'unconscious fantasy' in so far as it is conceived in its actuating as experience. Though he proclaims himself to be a Marxist, Sartre's criticism of modern Marxism is similar in the sense that he considers it has undergone certain deformities with mechanistic and idealistic thinking and has suffered a 'methodological sclerosis'; that in becoming monistically materialistic, it denies any dialectical relationship betweeen being and thought – thought being absorbed into being therefore loses its dialectical dynamism, becomes paralysed as it were. The Marxist dialectic of nature invents a nature without man. In the name of monism, the practical rationality of man making history is replaced by the blindness of natural accessibility.

In approaching groups, Sartre sees that it is through conflict entering inside a person or a group that history is made as a totalization of totalizations. He does not wish to be dogmatic or too theoretical, but considers that hyper-empiricism rejects everything *a priori* – and that on the contrary there is no reason why research should not be informed by principles. Dialectic reason has nothing to do with the forces presumed to operate in the realm of physics and chemistry. The idea of dialectics has arisen in history in quite another way, and has been discovered and defined in it through the relations of man to matter and of man to man, and not by a monism which is taken to govern human history from the outside.

Dialectical materialism is a school of philosophy founded by Marx and Engels, and has certain affiliations with Hegel's method of the triadic dialectics of thesis, antithesis and synthesis which, incidentally, were terms he did not use, but used instead 'affirmation', 'negation', and 'negation of negation'. By this dialectic, Hegel hoped to reconcile the age-long subject/object dualism. He gave as example the classical case of an authoritative regime (thesis), provoking the use of the antithesis (revolution), which evolves in the course of time to a synthesis of democratic moderation, etc. Marx turned this form of interpreting history upside down by pointing out that it was not ideas which were the propelling force in history, but matter and economics – historical materialism. Matter, nature, is taken without reservation as real in its own right, not deriving any reality from any outside, supernatural, or transcendental source, for example not from the mind of man. On the contrary, matter is prior to mind, which only appears as an epiphenomenon or outgrowth of matter. Dialectic expresses a dynamic interconnection of things, the universality of change, its radical nature, undergoing a continual process of self-transformation which manifests certain recurrent patterns, and which takes on three main forms, namely:

(1) The interpenetration, amity and strife of opposites – everything consisting of complexes of opposing elements and forces – a changing unity. Here again appears the conundrum of the relationship of the one (unity) to the many (opposing elements).
(2) The transformation of quantity into quality, for instance water, after a certain quantity of heat, alters its quality from liquid to gas, in a sudden transition or leap, in contrast to the gradualness of quantitative change – precipitating new qualities.
(3) The negation of negation – the new quality or synthesis contains a contradiction itself and so the spiral continues on a different qualitative level. The soul of the individual is acknowledged, but only as a sensitive organism responding to the

movement of underlying forces. Such an approach is reflected by Dorothy Stock Whitaker when she says that the development of a therapy group, from its inception to its termination, is characterized by the recurrence of basic themes under progressively expanding cultural conditions.

In both Hegelianism and Marxism, the final synthesis (which in Marxism starts off a new cycle) is the 'whole' to which the facts or elements in conflict relate in 'sublating' or resolving.

Quite clearly these ideas bear a resemblance to the concept of wholeness in the gestalt and field theories, and to the emerging patterns described in group dynamics, for example the recurrence of basic themes under progressively expanding cultural conditions. In both these examples, the sum of the elements of the part, or figure or theme, adds up to something less than what is qualitatively different from the whole gestalt or group culture or background.

Sartre's classification of groups in terms of a dialectical spiral is interesting, but simplistic because he applies what he sees in large historical groups – political parties, revolutionary movements, class collectivities – to all groups. He describes various phases in group life – seriality, the group in fusion, organization and institutionalization. He attempts the difficult task of integrating man as an existential being with the philosophy of Marx. He considers modern Marxism has completely forgotten the meaning of what a human being is, and to make up for this lack, 'it has nothing left but the absurd psychology of a Pavlov'.

Sartre calls his own attempt to integrate his Pour Soi with Marxist institutionalization the 'progressive-regressive method', that it is not merely a man's past which determines his attitude to the future, but his future (progression) plans and fantasies determine his attitude to the past. Therefore in that sense men are not passively, mechanically determined. He endorses fully a thesis Engels once made in a letter to Marx, namely that 'men themselves make their history, but in a given environment which conditions them', (there is dialectical interaction between the one and the many).

With regard to groups, he describes two social entities: (1) the group which aims at a definite purpose and in an organized way pushes towards the elimination of all inertia within itself; (2) the seriality, which is characterized on the contrary by its passive, inert, inorganic quality, a collective entity. The seriality is only very loosely structured – as with people in a bus queue, a cinema audience, etc.

He describes how, by a dialectical process, based on identification amongst the members of the series – *rassemblement* – gradual pressures on a seriality can result in the sudden formation of a group in fusion (not unlike what Foulkes has termed the 'condenser response'). At this point a structuring and organization takes place, and in due course may become so structured and frozen as to become an institution with a recurrence of inertia and an impotence of individual freedom and an inability to alter, yet with all the appearances of authority.

Wilfred Desan considers Sartre has, in so emphasizing the Pour Soi in the group situation, revived again the old French Cartesian dichotomy which he and other phenomenologists and existentialists are striving to resolve – that the Pour Soi is the cogito in disguise, and that in so impressively creating and defending the Pour Soi, he has had to tear down the scaffolding of the intersubjective, of the gestalt in his fear of organicism, in his antipathy of the group being more and other than the individual; he has killed that status of the group and the intersubjective, and therefore is not a real Marxist.

Viewed from the aspect of group analytic psychotherapy I think it is possible, as we shall see, to integrate at times successfully this eternal dichotomy of the individual and the group, or alternatively this massifying seriality of a materialistic Marxist monism in the setting of a suitably selected discussion group. Sociology might very well have begun with the study of the small group – and I think this free, intimate conversation and communication in an essentially social setting, both avoiding suffocation by the inorganic non-dialectical seriality or 'thingness' of institutionalization on the one hand, and the chaos of 'Hell is other people' of complete idealistic freedom on the other. It may be to the possibility of such a social setting that Sartre refers when he says the individual seeks to utilize his own and everyone else's procedure in the group as a third, as a mediator and regulator. It is interesting that on the one hand Marx treats the individual as if he were a group, and Sartre treats the group as if it were an individual. Speaking from a view-point of great social stress in the French underground movement, when the individual was once again divorced from the community in an extreme form, Sartre sought to solve the problem by the curious procedure of treating the individual as if he were the whole of humanity, as if he were the entire group, and responsible for it. He assumed that in choosing for himself, the individual chooses for all men. He is as preoccupied as Thomist and Marxist alike in emphasizing, each according to his bias, the separateness of individual and society, either that it is history which makes the individual, or alternatively that it is the individuals (existence) who precede history (essence). For the group therapist, they inter-act if given the opportunity, and only appear as disparate entities when individual and group fail to achieve adequate intercom-munication, and it is precisely on this region that group therapy focuses its attention, and which we shall now examine in great detail in the following chapter.

Chapter IV
Communicational Perspectives

The spiral of structure, process and content appears to be applicable in the field of communication, information, and general system theory. An analogy between communication and the course of a river has been made – the river creates the structure of the river bed and in turn this structure canalizes the river in a process of closest possible interaction. Together these shape a map equivalent to content – the 'information' apparent at any one moment. Cautious analogizing has always been basic to any scientific research; because of the nature of 'assembly' which, as we have mentioned, is derived from the Anglo-Saxon word meaning 'thing', sociology, particularly the macrostructures, has been relatively accessible to, and analogies have been drawn from, the language of physical science, mathematics, modern physics and engineering.

In a reverse direction, Norbert Wiener used constructs borrowed from sociology to present his account of cybernetics to the general public. Communication has proved to be a major scientific vehicle for relating physical, psychological and cultural events within one system. Ruesch and Bateson have defined communication as consisting of all the processes by which people influence each other and said that all actions and events have communicative aspects as soon as they are perceived, that persons, animals, plants or objects all emit signals which when perceived convey messages to the receiver (whether conscious or not, at the moment of perception), whether man-to-man, man-machine, or machine-machine. 'Where people convene things happen' – wherever relatedness of entities is being considered we deal with matters of communication in which the acquisition and retention of information are paramount.

The classical Aristotelian approach was to isolate and analyse, to reduce to simple, lineal, unidirectional cause-effect chains on a time sequence of prior cause and present effect – the 'why' of single causation. Sociological structures have replaced this by complex reticulate circuits, by networks of field and system and process, appealing to timeless, simultaneous states of related variables of 'equifinality', of 'multifinality', that is of devious developmental routes leading to similar final results or of similar conditions leading to dissimilar end-states, ranging from past and present to future and marking a revolutionary conceptual shift of attention from energy to information flow. An analogy has been made of the difference between kicking a stone and kicking a dog. The former is displaced according to the amount of energy transferred; the latter according to the effects of information transmitted, namely the triggering off of a response related not in quantitative terms but in a qualitative characteristic way to the communicated information, that the dog bites.

For four centuries the causal approach excluded as unscientific any attempt to include any such phenomena as purposiveness or vitalism. This system or field approach has been described as the biggest single shift in thinking since Plato and Aristotle. It unites natural and social science, resolving problems of teleology, of the body-mind dichotomy, which constituted the great historical gulf between psychology and the mathematical, between human nature and the engineering sciences. In the structural approach of the earlier thinkers, short-lasting processes were treated as static everlasting states of structure, governed by organic determinants and by spatial co-ordinates such as rigid hierarchy, closed systems, and later of topology and topography.

Process, on the other hand, implies change along a temporal co-ordinate, as is evident in the sociocultural constellations which are infinitely more plastic, more complex and ephemeral than the organic, the organistic and the inorganic systems. 'We focus on the particularly fluid nature of the structure of sociocultural systems and the thin conceptual line between this "structure" and what is called "process"' (Buckley). The same writer points out that morphostasis is a term that covers equilibrium in physico-chemical systems, homeostasis in organisms, and 'steady state' or ritual in sociocultural systems. The higher psychological and sociocultural levels are characterized primarily by their morphogenic properties. They maximize organization *per se*, and rather than preserve a given fixed structure they typically create elaborate or changed structure as a prerequisite to remaining viable, on-going systems.

In relation to the philosophy of science, this scientific world view, the product of a constant dialectic between the constructs of physical and those of biological science, has led away from concern for inherent substance, quantities, and properties to a central focus on the principles of organization, regardless of what it is that is organized. Imbalance and structural elaboration, not equilibrium and homeostasis, are characteristic inherent features of socio-cultural systems. Lester Ward described evolution as a struggle for structure rather than for the survival of the individual organism. In the field of psychology Gordon Allport, looking at personality as an open system, has defined system as a complex of elements in mutual interaction.

Physical sciences using recording instruments which fixate the data, also structure it in such a way that quantitative measurement comes first and qualitative evaluation comes second, regardless of whether such intervention by observation interferes with the values of what is being observed. Social science has to perform these functions simultaneously. Hence the engineers, in encountering the more complex patternings of mechanical and electronic devices, had to turn to sociology for some of their constructs, marking a significant *rapprochement* across the two-culture split. As we have said, Wiener chose the analysis of society to illustrate his cybernetic concepts. The one-way traffic from physical to behavioural science has ended, and a spiral of structure, process and content representing so many punctuations in open as distinct from closed systems would seem to present a more feasible model.

During the early thirties the Austrian mathematician and logician Gödel hit upon an inevitable inconsistency and incompleteness in any system of statements, that a statement cannot *be* self-contained in the sense of explaining its own axioms and not be self-contradictory. Any attempt to build a coherent body of statements at several levels of abstraction must always end in paradox. A contradiction (similar to the Marxist contradiction inherent in previous syntheses) is inherent in the very field of our enquiry. Gödel's conclusions are based on a study of Russell's group of paradoxes concerning 'the class of all classes which are not members of themselves'. Russell resolved this by introducing his theory of logical types – that whatever involves all of a collection cannot be one of the collection; which would suggest a hierarchical system, and defines here the paradox and dilemma of a group of individuals.

In group situations and for all systems of communication this inconsistency becomes a matter of considerable practical significance, whether for the sanity of the individual or for the viability of families and societies – indeed for the destiny of the world. For example, at a time when continued communication is most urgently needed, nations adopt a different level of communication, they 'break off relations' and go to war.

In communication theory two levels of communication are involved – the communication itself (for example an actual territory), and communication about communication (for example a map of that territory), or metacommunication. Metacommunication is an inherent quality of 'insight' and might also be seen as a contemporary formulation of the One in relationship to one. Contradiction can be denied by closing a system or a level of abstraction, by adopting rigidly hierarchical stratifications, or by imposing axiomatic moral injunctions from a higher level which put an end to further discussions and close the matter. We see a similar pattern in the watertight and compartmentalized disciplines of the various branches of science. In the small-group situation the whole intrapsychic organization becomes reorganized, the barriers between the various internal hierarchical levels (for instance the fixed classical topography of super-ego, ego, and id) become lifted and penetrable. Metacommunication is a way of transcending barriers to intercommunication by bringing the metacommunicational perspectives or context to bear on an intercommunicational dilemma, (such as a neurotic symptom), similar perhaps to the phenomenon Foulkes has described as 'locating'.

Psychotherapy is primarily a method of improving communication both intraphysically and in relation to others, and is essentially a metacommunicational system which leads to awareness of self in relationship to others, of consciousness which perhaps arises from these, and of the 'third order premise' of the perception of being perceived which leads to insight, where interpersonal communication is an intermediary towards intrapersonal understanding, though as Ruesch and Bateson have put it, interpersonal communication is often a very impoverished way of appreciating the richness of the intrapersonal world. The choice to focus upon the mirror of consciousness or the decision as to what is made conscious (which is itself unconscious), arises from intersubjectivity; for interpersonal relatedness perhaps this is what *con*sciousness refers to, not unrelated therefore, to *con*science. 'Insight' presupposes that 'outsight' exists. This selecting of what is to remain unconscious, repressed, and what is to be conscious, has no unconscious mind – it has no individual mind at all, but is essentially socially determined.

Intrapersonal processes are distinctly different from the events of the external world, and the constructs of codification refer to this difference, forming a translation and reflection of external events – the substitution of one type of event for another such that the event substituted shall in some sense stand for the other. In the computerization of communication this can be seen in terms of three distinct models, namely, first, the enumerative or digital, secondly, the directly recognizable or analogic, and thirdly, the contextual or gestalt system of wholes.

Structure as such tends to be imposed from the external environment, and is a system which results from this imposition, leading to interaction and creating patterns or organization of an 'internal' environment. Since environment must be external and cannot be internal, this is treated by the established *in*stitution of the structure as a further external *im*position; it is exposed as, for instance, is the threatening subculture such as a student movement – locked out or locked in – as the case may be. The viability of a structure depends on its capacity to assimilate these external impositions – to make use of its own deviances, via loop systems of feedback of information and servomechanisms as essential to self-regulation and self-correction. Perhaps this process of totalization plays a crucial role in establishing consciousness in the individual of unconscious, 'neurotic' manifestations, hence the significance for psychotherapy of a unified theory in the behavioural sciences including cybernetics, of which the small group setting is the paradigm, where the deviant, the neurosis, the idiosyncratic, the unique, the individual, the silent member or silent majority, offers the essential answer to a group dilemma. When a dyadic inter-communication dilemma between two people has proved insoluble 'the game without end', or has escalated to crisis proportions, it may respond to the presence of a third person (metacommunication), which constitutes therefore the smallest group possible, a group of three.

In the years following World War II, the significant change in the whole theoretical structure of the behavioural sciences occasioned by cybernetics, automation, computerization, communication and information theory provided us with entirely new, more rigorous, yet more flexible models. In all the major scientific fields, research flowered into the multidisciplinary realm of general or modern systems theory, and in sociology, in the open, complex sociocultural adaptive systems, as distinct from the previous more naïve and structured social system approach. The latter was essentially static, inflexible and insulated within its frameworks – less open to 'morphogenesis', but had nevertheless replaced, as we have noted, closed mechanical equilibria, or organic homeostatic models by more flexible, open shapings.

Science proceeds at the three levels of empirical research, logico-deductive theory and models or philosophies. It is the latter category which concerns general systems theory. The search for pattern in sequences of symbols, for 'stochastic' processes (or aims), forms the foundation for all scientific investigation. Where there is pattern, there is significance, there is 'meaning', but patterns are usually less subject to conscious inspection. The rules about language are distinct from language itself; for example, the abstract meaning of dependency may be less obvious than repeated demands for help. In the politico-economic sphere, the tangible 'means of production' are more readily grasped than the intangible abstractions of economics, of distribution and high finance.

These principles have been in the wind for several centuries. Vieta, for instance, during the eighteenth century became interested in algebraic relational variables, in function irrespective of magnitude, (geometry for measurement, and arithmetic for counting) and there is a parallel between this functional approach in mathematics and in the set theory of modern mathematics and the awakening of interest in psychology to concepts of relationship.

Now whilst mathematics possesses two languages, namely

symbolic (numerical and algebraic) to express mathematics *per se*, and natural language to express matters about mathematics, namely metamathematics, we have only natural language for both communication and metacommunication, which latter concerns the patterns of interaction and relationship. Failure to distinguish between these levels may lead to paradox, confusion and disaster.

Whilst it has been said that psychology is self-reflexive – subject and object are identical – this is even more true of social psychology, where the socius of self and others is taken as the unit for study. The essential relevance of this has arisen in the study of schizophrenia, which has been regarded in two distinct contexts – the one as an insulated incurable progressive disease of the individual mind, and the other, as the only possible response to an absurd, untenable, paradoxical, and confused communicational context, such as the double bind, or a particular family network.

A single communicational unit, namely a message, does not of itself communicate and the individual, unless he shares with another, does not originate communication. It is only in participation that communication occurs, that information is transmitted. In other words, the message only becomes a communication as a result of participation, in which it carries a social, or group, or relational, that is to say a metacommunicational, aspect. In computer language, the actual message is referred to as the abstract (abstracted from relational context), neural, numerical or *digital* mode of communication, and the other aspect, the relational or metacommunicational, as the humoral algebraic or analogic mode (it has a direct analogous equivalent in human relational terms). Whilst digital language is verbal, analogic language is non-verbal, and is concerned with quantity, quality and relationship. Human beings are the only organism known to use both analogic and digital modes of communication (with the possible exception of the dolphin). Digital language has a complex logical syntax, but lacks adequate semantics or meaningfulness in the field of relationship, while analogic language (sign language or onomatopoeic words) possesses meaningfulness, but lacks adequate syntax for unambiguous definitions of that meaning. Digital communication can be seen in secondary process phenomena, and analogic is roughly equivalent to the primary process. To summarize:

Analogic Metacommunication:	*Digital Communication:*
Primary process	Secondary process
Archaic sign language	Verbal
Non-verbal communication	Arithmetic quantities
qualities e.g. Kinesics, posture,	Abstract, logical
gesture, facial expression, mood	
signs, voice inflections, cadence,	
timing, rhythm, sequence	
Has more general validity,	Describes and explains
concerns relationship, empathy,	objects, and deals with the
and understanding	content of knowledge and
	transmission of knowledge
Has to do with meaning and	
intention of movements	
Semantic – matters of 'why'	Syntactical – matters of 'how'
Ambiguous	Can account for negative values
No distinction between past,	Observes spatio-temporal
present, and future, between	perspectives
temporal and spatial perspectives,	
eternal	
Humanistic	Mechanistic

Communication theory conceives of a symptom as a non-verbal message – as analogic. Patients suffering from schizophrenia behave as if they were trying not to participate, since their attempts at participation have not been treated as authentic or sincere. A discrepancy between digital and analogic communication has occurred in their participation, so that what has been said and what was meant appear to have been inconsistent and incongruous. They distort (paranoid), they withdraw (hebephrenic), or they evince total surrender (catatonic), as different ways of coping with these discrepancies, which appear as imperviousness to consistent communication alias participation. Art forms, ritual, myth, and neurotic symptoms are intermediaries between analogic and digital communication. Jung has shown that symbol appears where what the communication theorists would term 'digitalization' is not yet possible.

Modern or general systems theory, as already mentioned, attempts to extend this research to discover patterns and common constructs of a general nature, like an algebra of science, in communication, cybernetics and games theory, etc. Leading exponents in this field are Ludwig von Bertalanffy in *An Outline of General System Theory* (1950); Hall and Fagen, *Definition of System* (1956); James E. Miller, *Living Systems; Basic Concepts; Structure and Process; Cross Level Hypotheses* (1965); Walter Buckley, *Sociology and Modern Systems Theory* (1967). System has been defined as a set of objects, together with relationship between the objects and their attributes; objects are the components, attributes their properties, and relationship ties the whole system together.

These writers have been interested in regarding objects not in terms of, in the case of human beings, their intrapsychic attributes, but rather in terms of their communicational behaviour; an analogy with Skinner's 'black box' has been made from the field of telecommunications. In this instance, captured enemy electronic equipment was not opened up for investigation since this destroyed the internal structure, and only the knowledge of the function of this device in the greater system of which it was a part, was essential. Psychotherapists and certainly psychoanalysts, of course, cannot and do not let matters rest at that, since it is only by taking that content fully into account that the alienated outsider's inner world can be given the validity that is an essential feature of the deviant feedback loop. For instance, in group therapy, the scapegoatism – imperviousness theme produces the 'outsider' who makes essential pioneer links with the outside environment whether this be external to the group, or internal to the individual, (which is also treated by the group as external).

For the investigation of electronic apparatus under conditions of political urgency, the 'black box' approach may be expedient but in the highly sensitive setting of group psychotherapy it would be inconsistent with the true and full cross-fertilization between the perspectives of social structure and personal experience, which is considered here to be the key factor in therapy – of relating the One to one. Participation consists, therefore, not only of direct verbal messages as units of communication, but also of relationships and roles and 'role strains' which are reflected in the light of these communications – that is, metacommunications.

Hall and Fagen have described the essential aspects of environment for a given system – the set of objects which affect and are affected by the system to which the system, if it is to remain viable, must remain permeable, in the sense of osmosis, and 'open' with a resulting exchange of materials, energies, and information. This 'openness' of systems has freed science from the exclusively closed systems of classical physics and chemistry. Systems can, as has already been mentioned, relate or fail to relate vertically or hierarchically on different levels or horizontally, as in the serialization of departmentalism or compartmentalism. They have characteristics of wholeness, entitivity, of complexity, of non-summativity (the parts amount to more than their sum), and there are many essential contrasts between individually orientated approaches and communication theory. Interaction is non-summative, so that as the parts of a system are not related summatively or unilaterally, they must be related through a network or matrix of two-way multilateral circuitry. The sterile choice between deterministic and teleological causal sequences is outmoded – on-going 'here and now' phenomena play as important a role as 'there and then' etiological tracings to origins. The open system is its own best explanation, in contrast to the closed system which is predetermined by initial circumstances.

The metaphor of Plato, who considered that many participate imperfectly in the perfect nature of the Idea or Form, and that many are made in the imitation of the One, of Hobbes's *Leviathan* can now be given a more literalistic interpretation. In the general systems perspective, the emphasis is not upon whether matter is living or non-living, inorganic or organic, sensible or insensible, but upon the way in which these materials are organized, culminating in the fusion of organicism and mechanism. Ross Ashby points out that the older analytic Laplacian technique has been replaced by a holistic approach. The way not to approach a complex system is by analysis, for if we take it to pieces, we may not be able to reassemble it. Equilibrium is a term which applies to closed mechanical systems. For biological systems to avoid the static connotations of equilibrium, Cannon coined the term 'homeostasis' to bring out the basically dynamic, precessual, unstable but relatively constant properties of physiological systems with their continuously varying condition. Finally the term 'steady state' or 'morphastasis' has been coined by Walter Buckley, referring to the extreme plasticity that characterizes sociocultural systems – far exceeding the plasticity of organisms, yet contriving to remain viable, indeed thriving upon change and exchange, and 'running down' similar to the construct of positive entropy if closed and insulated, undergoing therefore, a continuous cycle of structuring, destructuring, restructuring, constructing, at increasingly complex levels.

The mechanistic school of social physics of Comte which so proudly replaced the vitalism, teleology, mysticism and anthropomorphism of previous eras, the organic metaphors of Spencer, the social and rational mechanisms of Pareto, the organismic model of Lilienfeld, the social space systems in equilibrium, of closed boundaries, of centrifugal and centripetal forces, of consensus and conflict constellations of Lewin and of the group dynamicists generally, have only very clumsy, unwieldy and crudely operable models for psychotherapists to work with.

Lester Ward was one of the first to see the fundamental difference between organism and the principles of sociocultural organization – emphasizing 'knowledge-attaining processes' and the 'struggle for structure', and the place of 'synergy' in the 'systematic working together of the antithetical forces in nature to produce organization'. The Chicago school of Small, Mead and Park, stimulated principally by the work of Simmel and Von Wiese, opened the closed system of structured mechanical organismic models in favour of open process models, which were congenial to and even anticipated the basic principles of cybernetics. Others who shared this process view of reality were Marx, Whitehead, Einstein, Dewey, Bentley and Cooley, who saw social interaction as a continuous process of socialization, or in the case of Cooley, of humanization, as distinct from the mere enactment of social forces. Closed systems are structures that increase steadily in entropy and finally run down, are destroyed by intrusion from the environment, whilst the open systems decrease in entropy and are therefore viable and perpetuated rather than becoming sclerosed as if with old age by a 'heavy cake of tradition'.

Mechanical systems are expressed in the physical terms of

energy, flow and power, whilst complex adaptive systems negotiate matters in the light of information and legitimate authority. Dewey and Mead as distinct from Parsons considered structure as being continuously opened and restructured by the problem-solving behaviour of the individual experiencing and responding to concrete situations – in other words, participating in the meaning for the individual of that particular structure. Cognition therefore involves social structure not merely as an empty category, but as a vital process involving the dynamic assessment of the situation and of the relations between self and others which transposes and refocuses therefore, from decision-making to role strain and games theory. Parsons has been criticized for failing to give sufficient significance to deviance through non-conformity (for example newcomers), which in the general systems approach is welcomed since systems thrive on the feedback from the disturbances, variety and the information which these provide, and is the very substance of creativity, elaboration and viability. Paradoxically one-sided social control, institutionalism and anthropomorphism destroys the man (as long ago recognized by Aristotle).

The structured, rigidly closed system relies on the energy flow of force, coercion, and power imposed from the outside without agreement rather than upon information 'exposed', disclosed from within. Whilst structure can be viewed as bound *energy*, organization is an expression of bound *information*, which once realized by the individual, in the form of feedback loops, triggers off structural effects, such as the linking that one sees in a newly constituted group brought about by one member from a previous group. In psychoanalysis the transference with its resort to manipulation or seduction is an example of coercion, adopted in order to avoid the threat and anxiety of information.

The following diagram is borrowed from Walter Buckley's *Sociology and Modern Systems Theory*, and illustrates succinctly the three models of equilibrium, homeostasis, and morphostasis:

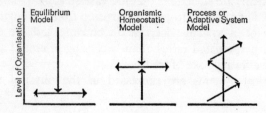

The following schema serves to elaborate the diagram:

Equilibrium	*Homeostasis*	*Morphostasis*
Closed mechanical System. Minimally adaptive and minimally organized. Relatively closed boundaries shaped by external pressures.	Organismic System. Relatively high level of organization. Boundaries less closed; 'semi permeable', surrounding a constant but changing internal environment	Sociocultural System. Systems model with highly adaptive, elaborate and evolving organization, openly and freely transacting with the environment by adaptive processes, with complex open boundaries, 'morphogenic.'

The way, therefore, that general systems theory regards the various scientific disciplines is in terms of varying degrees of systemness, entity, and integration, e.g. nuclear particles, atoms, molecules, solar systems, cells, organisms, ecological communities, societies, sociocultural patterns, as distinct from summativity or the sum of parts in unorganized aggregates, for instance serialization. Whilst the relation of parts in a physiological organism involved complex physio-chemical energy, the relationship of parts in sociological contexts is primarily of a psychic nature, involving processes of exchange of information and communication summed up in the psychosociological notions of Tarde that the individual is truly social and society is truly psychical and does not consist of a split between individual and society, studied as separate closed entities. In the pre-cybernetic machine, the designer had to anticipate and exclude all contingencies and countermeasures from the machine as distinct from the modern concept of a machine which uses these very contingencies as sources of self-regulating information called servomechanisms, (such as the thermostat), which are fed back into the machine with considerable gain in capability and which steer and govern the whole machine.

Self-direction in the sociocultural adaptive system receives information from three sources – from the environment, from itself and its parts, and from the past. Correspondingly, there are three sorts of feedback, namely goal-seeking from external data, self-awareness of consciousness from internal data, and learning from the past; and three sorts of function, namely, a total group goal, preservation of and satisfaction for the individual, and preservation of the group. The polar opposites of a system range through a continuum from chaos and complete randomness at one end to environmental constraint at the other.

In the same way that Heidegger made a plea for a return of philosophy to metaphysics, the study of being, particularly human being as such, so a plea has been made in sociology to bring men back in again, for an increased attention to the psychological factors of the individual as providing the essential deviant feedback information of intervening variables such as language in social explanation. In an article 'Aspects of language and learning in the genesis of the social process' (1961), Basil Bernstein has put it that

'A major theoretical problem is the relationship between the social structure and individual experience. Through what means is the social process learnt and what are the implications of such learning? These questions raise critically the problem of the relationship between sociology and psychology. The sociologists' attempt to derive personality statements is often considered by the psychologists as crude and insensitive, whilst to the sociologist, psychological statements relating to social process, particularly to institutional behaviour, have an air of joyous *naïveté*. It seems that neither discipline has reached a level of theoretical sophistication such that integration becomes possible. An approach to two questions may be made if one examines an intervening variable which is limited and shaped by a given type of social organization, and yet conditions the form of a basic learning process. I would like to examine the possibility that spoken language, or rather specific linguistic terms, fit these criteria.'

He goes on to divide language into public concrete or restricted language, and formal or elaborated language (which perhaps bears certain similarities with analogic and digital communication).

The perennial 'locus' problem of social psychology is based on a coupling of organism and organization in a single system. Meaning is generated during this total transaction and does not reside in the intradermal or intracranial self or personality alone. Mead, in *Mind, Self and Society* (1934), has put it that

'The field of mind must be co-extensive with and include all the components of the field or social process of experience and behaviour, i.e. the matrix of social relations and interactions among individuals. . . .' 'If mind is socially constituted, then the field of locus of any given individual mind must extend as far as the social activity or apparatus of social relations which constitutes it extends; and hence that field cannot be bounded by the skin of the individual system to which it belongs.'

Information lies not just in the individual nor in stored records, but is found in the changing topology of the social pathways to communication, and whilst meaning remains a strictly individual and intrapsychic experience, information resides in the total psychosociological mapping. The tracings of these mappings are reflected in the experience of the individual participants and range somewhere along a continuum between social security and personal freedom. Walter Buckley has devised two schemata applying to two social cultural patterns, legitimate authority and coercive power respectively:

I. Legitimate Authority
   (Information Flow)

II. Coercive Power
   (Energy Flow)

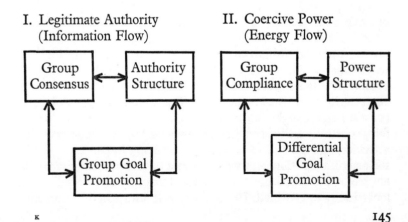

What are the factors promoting morphogenesis from one of these systems to the other – from II to I, for instance, which for most group therapists, at any rate, would probably be regarded as a therapeutic ploy? The answer probably is along the lines suggested in the final chapter – namely, in actively creating the structure – that is, in providing in the first place the setting, the facilities, the selection, the arrangements, the opportunities, the time, the place, and the members themselves, the 'locus'; in the second place, allowing the processes of communication to emerge in this structure, that is, playing a relatively less active role in catalyzing these processes; thirdly, in leaving the content to define itself, to create its own metastructure, in which the therapist plays a relatively passive role and refrains from making interventions. The untenable paradox of being made to be spontaneously democratic is resolved by providing this hierarchically tiered but relatively open circular or spiral system.

Berger and Luckman in their book *The Social Construction of Reality* (1967) have described two sociocultural systems which they term primary and secondary socialization, a term coined by Max Scheller, during the 'vertigo of relativity' of the 1920s. They are concerned with the sociology of knowledge, with the relationship between human thought and its social context, a root proposition powerfully introduced by Marx into modern social thought, namely, that man's consciousness is determined by his social being, the economic substructure playing a dialectical role with the reflexive superstructure of consciousness.

They proceed to develop the theme of socialization, and point out that man occupies a peculiar position in the animal kingdom, since he has no species-specific environment, no environment firmly structured by his own instinctual organization, in the manner that animals live in closed worlds predetermined by their biological equipment. By contrast, man's relationship to his environment is characterized by world openness. The drives of his biological constitution are highly unspecialized and undirected and can therefore, constitutionally speaking, cope with a highly plastic range of activities, and are still so developing, referring in particular to his sociocultural development which cannot be understood in terms of his biological constitution alone. His humanity and sociality are inextricably intertwined. Homo Sapiens is always and in the same way, Homo Socius. The social order is not part of the 'nature of things'. It cannot be derived from the 'laws of nature', and exists only as a product of human activity. The formation of the self, therefore, must also be understood in relation not only to his ongoing organismic development, but also to social process in which the natural human environment is mediated by the currency of language in which conversation in particular plays so vital a role.

Berger and Luckman suggest that the most important vehicle of reality maintenance is conversation that can afford to be casual, that the reality of everyday life presents as the participant intersubjective social world that is shared with others and which becomes the objective repository of a vast accumulation of meaning and experience preserved in time and transmitted to later generations. They make the point that the institutional (highly structured) world is experienced as an objective reality (the external environment), that this reality is precarious (open to restructuring, that is, in a state of morphostasis open to morphogenesis), that all societies are constructing in the face of chaos, are an attempt at objectification, institutionalization and legitimation, and that there is a continuous dialectical process between individual and society, between personal identity and social structure, between individual existence and social reality (between one and One). They make a plea for society to have its place in the company of the sciences that deal with man as man, as a humanistic discipline, and see society in a dialectic of externalization (via conversation), of objectivation (via intersubjectivity) and of internalization, equivalent to personal meaningful experience. The reality of everyday life is the objectivating intersubjective world, structured spatially, temporally and socially – all three of which constitute the intrinsic properties of human consciousness.

They describe primary socialization as occurring during childhood, by which the individual becomes a member of society through the 'significant others', who are emotionally speaking highly charged and over whom there is no choice. Secondary socialization consists of any subsequent process which 'inducts' an already (primarily) socialized individual with new sections of the objective institution or world of his society, when the dialectic is between identification by others and self-identification, of institutionally based 'subworlds' expressed in role-making, which are rooted in such matters as divisions of labour and carry role-specific vocabularies. The transition between primary and secondary socializations is accompanied by a legitimating apparatus, for example ritual (such as initiation ceremonies) and material symbols. A second language has to be learned in the form of various idioms as distinct from one's 'mother tongue', and in the process of the transition art forms such as music play an intermediary role between these two languages, which are emotionally loaded and intense identification occurs legitimately as with the *maestro* for instance, equivalent to primary identification with the significant others of the family. There is a decline in the role of the family in relation to secondary socialization in the form of such rituals as initiation and various other specific social sanctions, strictures and taboos such as ridicule, which are created to offset the development of reality-disintegrating doubts.

Problems of inconsistency between the original and the new internalizations occur, since there is the already formed self and the already internalized world of primary socialization. (In psychotherapy, particularly group psychotherapy, one sees this very clearly when for instance an adolescent girl feels that to participate in the group is putting on an act, is vaguely unreal and insincere and self-conscious, and that the only real setting is that in relationship to her mother.) Whilst primary socialization cannot take place without stabilizing first this emotionally charged identification, most secondary socialization can afford to dilute this and proceed effectively with only the amount of identification that enters into any communication – for instance it is not necessary to love one's teacher like one's mother (but when this does occur in relationship to the psychotherapy, this forms the basis for either transference or replacement therapy.)

In primary socialization, the child does not see the significant others as institutional functionaries, but as mediators of reality *per se* and internalizes the world of the parents as *the* world, and not as a specific institutional context. The crises (such as adolescence) that occur after primary socialization are caused by the (often frightening) recognition that the parents' world is *not* the only world, and has a very specific (limited) social location. The role of the others in secondary socialization carries a high degree of

COMMUNICATIONAL PERSPECTIVES

anonymity, readily detached from the individual performers, for instance seriality, replaceability, interchangeability, formality.

Re-socialization (such as occurs in group psychotherapy) is based on the reality of the 'here and now' setting of the group, and re-interprets and bridges the hiatus and inconsistencies between the primary socialization of the past and the secondary socialization of the past and present.

Gregory Bateson, in an article 'Cultural Problems posed by a study of Schizophrenic Process' (1959), concerning field work he carried out in New Guinea, sees a whole culture placed in the paradox or 'double bind'. From its own point of view, the culture faces either external extermination or internal disruption, and the dilemma is so constructed as to be a dilemma of self-preservation in the most literal sense. In the culture he describes, two processes are at work, the first of symmetrical rivalry (competition), the second of complementary themes, for instance domination-sub-mission, exhibition-spectatorship, succouring-dependence, sado-masochism. The hypothesis was that the culture maintained a psychological equilibrium by a balancing of these two contrary processes, either of which by itself would lead to disruption, and neither of which is communication 'on the level'.

This leads back to the problem of paradox, which should now be considered in the light of the small psychotherapy group setting. The structure of a newly constructed group is essentially a paradox-ical situation. Basically paradox is incommunicability. The group, like a statement, starts as a paradox. The group circle is itself a system composed of individual components who, through a communication and metacommunication, re-shape by a process of 'morphogenesis' a metastructure according to the information it emits, and which is experienced by the individual as having a particular meaning characteristic of that particular metastructure (or content, as we have called it), at that particular place and moment.

Paradox has been defined as a contradiction following correct deduction from consistent premises that produces self-contra-diction by accepted ways of reasoning. Simple contradiction, however, involves choice and paradox and is not simply a set of mutually exclusive alternatives because, like the double-bind, paradox renders choice itself impossible, for example, 'Be spontaneous!'. The basis for a solution to the patterns of all paradox is that no change can be generated from within a closed system. Any morphogenesis can only come from stepping outside the pattern by establishing contact with another open system, thereby punctuating the 'game without end' of a neurosis, or of a neurotic relationship. Such 'stepping outside' as waking up out of a nightmare state or invoking therapeutic intervention evolves new emergent systems of higher complexity. Levels of knowledge, like levels of metastructuring, have been postulated with first, second, third, and even fourth-order patternings, such as 'I perceive you', 'You perceive me perceiving you', 'I perceive you perceiving me perceiving you', etc., involving areas of intuition and empathy, even the escalating levels of love, which includes all these and more, and is similar to Laing's seeing the task of social phenomenology as the study of the relation between experience and experience – 'its true field is inter-experience'. What we need to ask ourselves is always and at whatever moment, what it is that is preventing this – for example is it apparent from the content of what is being said that primal-scene sadistic fantasies are preventing participation as being too frightening? Neurotic states, paranoid, depressive, manic, obsessional, anxiety, hysterical, addictive, and phobic states are all closed systems. Communication re-opens them; participation cures them. They are all states that have been taken over as splinters from some other previous or current group, and it is in this sense that mentation has been mistakenly ascribed to the group. In fact it is the other way round, that groups in panic, in states of persecutory violence, in fragmentation, in disaster, leave their imprint in little insulated lacunae within the individual mind, as we see to this day in those 'exhaustion cases' of traumatic experiences from the last and even the previous World War. The totalization of all these lacunae becomes projected into the group setting and creates the group climate at any one particular moment in the 'here and now' group state.

This is an area of primary significance in psychotherapy involving insight, reflexiveness, empathy, love, of higher and higher levels of abstraction of inexpressible metacommunications, for example the real, verified, manifestation of a hysterical system such as an actual headache as distinct from the euphemistic 'headache' used as an excuse to withdraw from a social commitment.

These levels of thinking, for example 'sophistication', are of paramount importance as criteria in selecting members for a psychotherapeutic group. The confusion, the frustration, the time-wasting that occurs because members of a group are not on the same wavelength, and live and communicate at different levels of metacommunication, speaking different idioms as if they were speaking foreign languages, must be enormous. There is considerable need to assess these matters in terms of some sort of optimal degree and distance, since neurosis here too plays a significant role and makes its indefinable contribution, so that in this area we are dealing to some extent with a question that begs itself.

In groups, the essence of therapy lies not in communicating, not in understanding or responding, not in reacting, interacting, or transacting, not in experiencing *per se*, but in meaningful participation.

People therefore suffering from these states of depression or paranoia or panic complain not of something but of nothingness, which has a peculiar, unendurable quality worse than physical pain, with a loss of the sense of time and place – a timeless isolated quality and which is experienced as endless even though it lasts for only a split second, analogous to experiences of extreme sensory deprivation and which may possibly give rise, for example, to the starvation and yearning sensations seen in drug addiction.

Whilst with physical suffering sympathy from others is never short in coming, these psychological states elicit no empathy except by other sufferers, and no sympathy – rather do they qualify for non-comprehension, ridicule and boycott. As one adolescent girl described it: 'When I feel paranoid everyone laughs at me. I am ludicrous, a big joke. It's my hang-up, not theirs. It's not even unhappiness – only timeless, spaceless emptiness, loneliness and panic. Ordinary physical pain has an effect, something can be done. Even for the fish out of water, there is a way back, but in depression there is nothing – no emotion, only emptiness. When I think I could have been enjoying myself, it seems such a waste. I get a lost feeling, I may as well not be around' – reminiscent of Freud's description of the loss of object.

Group therapy tries to reverse this process; the fish is put back into the sea, the continuum is restored. How to create a viable, breathable medium is the question. Communication and the time to communicate which takes place in the bland solvent of casual conversation helps to untie the knotted threads of repression. The problem is not who, or what, or how, or to what effect communication takes place, but whether a medium *per se* for participation exists at all. It is the space between that is as important as the people themselves – the open system of the small group mindful of Einstein's observation that it is not the charges or the particles, but the field of the space between them, which is essential for the description of physical phenomena – a field that in physics is electromagnetic force and in human association is visuo-auditory information and contact. Let us now proceed to examine the perspectives of the small group itself.

Chapter V
Small Group Perspectives

In the preceding chapters, the perspectives of small group psychotherapy have been explored in their tripartite ramifications into psychosocial *structures*, into *processes* of communication, and thirdly in the *content* or patterns of meaning that have emerged in philosophy and general systems theory.

From sociology, the field theory and group dynamics of Kurt Lewin and the microfunctionalists have played a determining role. From psychology, psychoanalysis and gestalt psychology have shaped our attitudes, reflected in the adoption of the relatively non-directive role of the conductor, in the focusing on free-floating discussion, in the moulding of our understanding and interpretations, and in directing our attention to the total situation of the figure-background constellations.

Since World War II, communication and general systems theory has received added impetus from the field of cybernetics, where a revolutionary emphasis has been placed on information as distinct from energy (for example libido) flow. Finally, the metastructures created as content out of the highly activating setting of the group structure, facilitated to their ultimate extent by these processes of communication, evolve patterns bearing affiliations with certain ideas in philosophy, such as phenomenology and existentialism, the Eigenwelt, Mitwelt, Umwelt of Husserl, the Dasein of Heidegger, the 'relation' as distinct from the 'thing' concept of Cassirer, the 'truth is communicability' of Jaspers. This aspect of the group has particularly to do with socialization, with humanization, and with meaning.

These three aspects of the group, namely structure or the activating structure, processor communication, content or socialization, have received varying emphasis. For instance, the group dynamicists would seek to explore and utilize the setting or structure as their main therapeutic agency – for instance the sociogram of Moreno: they, as it were, treat the group *per se*, therapy *of* the group. Others focus upon the psychological, for instance, the psychoanalytic aspects, psychoanalysis *in* the group, for example Wender, Schilder, Slavson, Wolf and Schwartz.

Others, to varying degrees attempt judicious admixtures of gestalt and group dynamic, of psychological approaches, (usually psychoanalytic), of communication theory and of philosophy (for example Gregory Bateson, Don Jackson, Ronald Laing). They all variously study the relevance of these approaches in their interplay for psychotherapy, and their intention is to enable the group to learn how to handle its own tensions, how to undertake its own therapy – therapy *by* the group. The Tavistock group including or influenced by such writers as Rickman, Bion, Ezriel, Sutherland, Turquet, Gosling, Laing, and from a somewhat different direction Foulkes, have been called 'the British school of group dynamic analysts'. From the United States Bach, Ackerman, Scheidlinger, Durkin, Stock Whitaker, Reusch, Bateson, to name but a few, could be said to be varyingly representative of a similar orientation.

Foulkes's approach is interesting because he goes beyond analytic and Lewinian theory in his emphasis on communication theory and group phenomenology. Because of the comprehensiveness and less spectacular nature of his method, its uniqueness is sometimes overlooked. Its flexibility gives scope for development, for 'morphogenesis', and offers opportunity for observation of group processes *per se*, for a phenomenology of the group which is relatively free of the distortions and the artefacts which follow in the wake of more systematized formulations. The comprehensiveness of his approach is not so much characterized by the presence of unique features as by a broad spectrum of several factors. The influence of gestalt psychology and of field and communication theory are evident in his concept of the group matrix and of 'location', that the individual participants (foreground figures) operate against the background of a total network of communication or matrix which is a slowly developing specifically group phenomenon, in which the meaning of an individual neurotic response can be mapped out against its group context.

Classical psycho-analytical theory provides a fuller scope for understanding the processes being enacted in the group, and Foulkes was probably the first to recommend free-floating discussion or 'group association', equivalent to the free association of psychoanalysis. This he did as long ago as 1942. He made the proviso that the group situation modifies all psycho-analytic concepts by introducing these new, specifically group features. The sociologists have never in fact explored small groups with the detailed intensiveness of the group psychotherapist. The 'group mentality' of Bion, the 'group matrix' of Foulkes, the 'network of inter-group transferences based on a common fantasy' of Ezriel, all have affiliations with the group dynamics of Lewin. Although there is no coherent school of pure group dynamic theory as such, and most group therapists combine group dynamic with a recognized psychotherapeutic school of thought, usually psychoanalytically orientated, nevertheless they practically all look to group forces as a primary therapeutic agent, and consider that group dynamic features of the group as a whole constitute the new and determining ingredient.

In the United States, for at least two decades, these two approaches, dynamic and psychoanalytic, worked in relative disregard of each other, and by some workers the two had been assumed to be virtually incompatible, since the dynamic emphasized the 'phenotype', contemporaneous 'here and new' aspects of group as distinct from the 'there and then' genotype of psychoanalysis. Experimental psychology has also shown a progressive tendency towards emphasizing the 'here and now', present situation. The method of determining the properties of a situation by testing them at that particular moment in time avoids the uncertainties of historical conclusions. It does not follow, however, that the method eliminates considerations of time periods altogether. A 'situation at a given time actually does not refer to a moment without time extension, but to a certain time period. This fact is of great theoretical and methodological importance for psychology' (Lewin 1943). Viewed from today, there is no incompatibility – at the most it is a matter of emphasis only. As a member of a group recently remarked: 'If there were no past, there would be no need for a memory.'

There is also the fact that most of the specific researches dealing with group-determined phenomena, for example goals, structure, decision-making, cohesiveness, codes, values, climate, role-playing, are more relevant for groups involved with training, small classes, work, education, administration industry, selection, social work, counselling, mental hygiene, etc., as distinct from therapy, and that the principles involved had been too foreshortened and con-temporaneous, too broad, general and facile, too transient, too exteriorized, to be relevant for any but the crudest of therapeutic ploys. They have been gleaned from brief studies of groups in widely different settings – for example over very short periods of two weeks or so, (for instances street corner gangs), and therefore of a more ephemeral nature. Group analysts and therapists, on the contrary, work specifically and intensively with small, highly standardized groups over very long periods, which provide oppor-tunity for 'submicroscopic' observations and allow time for complex development and change, and include a greater inferential leeway in conceptual framework, as for instance in borrowing from psychoanalytic theory. In addition, in the group analytic groups, as distinct from other groups, there are the striking differences of technique and procedure. There is no direct external goal, no task, no programming. Once they have been formed, guidance and leadership are kept down to a minimal level, and there is the intro-duction of an entirely new sort of sociology, namely the study of 'therapeutic processes'. The group therapist has to be currently alive to individual, group and therapeutic processes when they cut across each other, or when they supplement or complement.

As long ago as 1937, the psychologist J. F. Brown was pointing out the essential compatibility of field and psychoanalytic theory, the supersummative and holistic (the person), the functional (the self-regulating qualities of the individual), and the dynamic (motivational) nature of both approaches. He drew attention to the fact that they both adopt bold hypothetico-deductive methods involving considerable theorizing and theoretical constructs.

The impulse to seek a *rapprochement* between dynamicist and analyst has come mainly from the group dynamicists, notably Lewin himself, Bates, Thelen, Peck, Stock Whitaker, Bennis and Benne, and Hill. On the other hand, a few of the leading American group analysts (Slavson, Wolf, Schwartz) have adopted the contrary view of reinforcing the cleavage but, in this, three very significant research findings have been those of Henry B. Peck, of Bennis and

Benne and of Thelen. Peck concluded that the small group was a possible means of bridging the gap between the psychoanalytic and the epidemiological point of view, and formulated the hypothesis of individual group psychological isomorphism (I.G.P.I.), namely, that the psychological organization of groups is fundamentally similar to that of individuals, though this does not mean they are identical.

His I.G.P.I. hypothesis has been well tested experimentally, although continued research is still needed. He views the small group as a psychological entity capable of activating its own purpose, behaviour, identity and relation with the outer environment and its own component units, and that group psychiatry and group dynamics are 'viable hybrids' capable of comprehending each other, though it is equally clear that an individual is not a group, nor is the group an individual.

Similarly Bennis and Benne (1958) at the National Training Laboratory, discovered and later confirmed with a wealth of empirical data, that the group goes through the same 'epigenetic' phases as does the individual, thereby bringing group psychology and group dynamics into close relationship, 'epigenetic' meaning a development involving a gradual diversification and differentiation from an initially undifferentiated entity (such as a stone or a rock which undergoes changes in universal character owing to outside influences). They describe groups as a whole regularly moving through preoccupations with authority to preoccupation with personal relationships, typically going through three sub-phases. The first centres round authority difficulties, submission, rebellion, independence; the second round problems of identification and self-identity and interdependence; in the third phase non-conflicted members take over leadership. These phases may overlap and may occur in cycles.

Investigations carried out by Preston and Heints (1949) for instance showed that changes of opinion in discussion groups were more easily brought about by means of participating than by supervisory leadership. Autocratic leadership may at times increase productivity, but decreases group morale and may, in the long run, also interfere with productivity.

Professor Herbert Thelen (1958), the social psychologist, has translated 'the vaguely worded abstractions of Bion' (*Experiences in Groups* 1948–1951) into operational terms and found they could be put to experimental test with a behavioural rating system. He confirmed that his 'work level' and 'basic assumptions' in the slightly different terms of 'work and emotionality' were scientifically observable, which was re-confirmed by W. F. Hill (1961). Whitman, Lieberman and Stock (1958–1962) worked on concepts of the group as a whole, and of the individual in terms of the group, and of the group in terms of the individual, in rateable terms.

Helen Durkin's views are that, since nothing can be proved if the design of the research is not rigorous, there should be a continued *rapprochement* in collaborative research between dynamicists and therapists with complementary implementation of each approach. The group therapist should turn to the group dynamicist as a consultant on research, design and methodology. Nevertheless, as an analyst, she finds it natural to extend the normal analytic process of transference towards the analyst to transference towards the group as a whole – along lines similar to Ezriel's. She also finds that the analytic approach provides valuable information of an essentially re-constructive nature. She goes beyond the phenomenological data and plumbs the depths of motivation involving a high degree of inference; otherwise she finds she is liable to miss the whole crux of the individual patient's pathological conflict.

To interpolate, it would seem that psychoanalytic information is like any other information which there seems no purpose in specifically excluding, particularly when the opportunity to use this information seems to present itself. The essence of the conflict, operationally speaking, is between the particular group climate that the patient is contributing towards and therefore helping to create, and what he regards as the forbidden aspects of himself – forbidden, in fact, by the atmosphere he has colluded with the other members in creating. One feels that if Freud had started his investigations using the small group setting rather than the individual's free associations on the couch, he might very well have arrived at his metapsychological conclusions earlier than he did, since themes from group associations are usually far less disguised, far more dramatically transparent than those derived from individual free associations.

Two questions come to mind. First, what are the equivalents, in group terms, of neurosis generally, of transference, repressions, regression, resistance? For instance, does a group of neurotics' behaviour differ radically, and in what way? Bion suggests that a group of neurotics is more liable to manifest basic assumption behaviour basically. Secondly – when, what, how and whose contribution does one interpret? The systematic consistent working through of 'deeper' nuclear conflicts in the individual setting would appear to be compensated for by the fact of their being more obvious, if not to the individual, at any rate to the other members of the group – hence the 'mirroring' possibilities – the 'insight' may be less, but must be contrasted with the sharability and availability of the 'outsight' provided by the group setting, which becomes transferable and exchangeable provided the atmosphere concocted by the members as a whole is conducive to doing so.

The nearest that Lewin approached a psychotherapy group was perhaps in the development of 'T groups' or Training Groups, which he initiated in the form of sensitivity training involving awareness and insight and the sensitivity towards and the emphasis on the experiencing and verbalization of feelings including those concerning personal relationship. Kurt Lewin, just before he died in 1947, established the Research Centre for Group Dynamics, officially located at the Massachusetts Institute of Technology. He was one of the research workers who instituted the beginnings of the first National Training Laboratories in the group development section of the American National Education Association which held its first session in Bethel, Maine, in 1947, though the title of National Training Laboratory was not used till 1951. The principle of the T group has spread very widely indeed, involving the field of education, industry and training generally. A manner of looking at T group theory is as a schema which ranges over a triangular area: at one angle is the work or W group, having a clearly defined external task such as education or recreation or some other specified goal; at the second angle is the psychotherapeutic or psychodynamic aspect, which is concerned primarily with the internal system of the individuals; the third angle represents the group *per se*, the social or group dynamic aspect of the interpersonal dimension, and of the relationships.

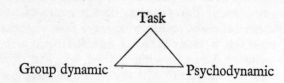

Somewhere between these three poles lies the T or training group, playing a triadic role with a task or goal on the one hand that is educational, industrial, social or administrative, and on the other (unlike work groups that have a specified external goal) with a cognizance and awareness of the psychological and group dynamic aspects that may be interfering with productive functioning of the group, for instance the processes of learning. The principle of the T group can be very widely applied in other situations such as the therapeutic community; for instance David Clark's book, published in 1964, was titled *Administrative Therapy*, which integrated administration with group psychotherapeutic principles.

At this point it might be helpful to conceptualize a schema similar to that employed in the chapter on sociology, in which the various group approaches could be located relative to each other and which could act as an operational guide through the complex happenings as they are actually encountered in conducting groups. The group situation is a convenient term for describing the entire field in which these events occur, and like sociology can be systematized under a triad of structure, process, and content. These correspond also with the three perspectives of communication, namely intrapersonal or monologue, the interpersonal or duologue, and the transpersonal or dialogue, and they relate to the three time perspectives of future, present, past, that is communi*cable*, communi*cating*, and communi*cated*.

(I) The structure of the group consists of the spatiotemporal constitution of the group itself, that is, the time, the setting, and the seating arrangements, early procedures, the declared goals and agenda, the members themselves, and their selection, the relatively constant framework of seven to eight members who are potentially communicative – communicable in the future – meaning being intrapersonal or appearing only as monologue.

(II) The group mediating processes are those of action, interaction, the on-going dynamic processes of behaviour, or relating and of communicating, of rituals, the 'atoms' of group acts, of duologues building up chains of interpersonal dialogue, of articulation.

(III) The content (which could also be termed its form in the sense of 'information') is the phenomenological, meaningful shape or organization of the group, the matrix of the total transpersonal network or channels which has been laid down or communi*cated* – the outcome of the previous two categories – the group's *metastructure*. The content is non-verbal in the sense that it has been communicated, and it takes on shape and meaning for the individual members implicitly, with the emergence of undeclared goals, which is reflected in their roles, patterns of relating to each other plus the shared, often prejudiced, attitudes of a group culture. Whilst the structure remains constant, it is the phenomenological intention or meaning for the individual of the metastructure or matrix which plays a role in altering the individual members 'intrapersonally', after which that particular cycle of events can be said to be completed. This is reminiscent of the Aristotelian notion of matter (in this instance the group structure) consisting of determinate potentialities that became actualized only through the activities of forms – or of Sartre, who considers that group organization (in this case group form) define group structure, and starts off a new cycle of events. In other words, as the primary structure of the group remains constant, it can only alter in a phenomenological sense in subjective meaning for the individual. It is thus the individual who changes, and must change intrapersonally in his personality at one and the same time, by having actively contributed towards and created the group content, its matrix, form, or metastructure.

To elaborate [on (I)], the group structure refers to the unchanging event of the small group itself, a collective of individuals, the homogeneous One and the constitutional plurality of the same people, same number, under similar conditions of time, duration, place arrangements and procedure with the multiplicity of the 'many', the 'one' of the individual who is the multiple for the others, a group of individuals. This antithesis of group and individual creates a tension which mobilizes interaction of varying degrees of intensity which can either unite or fragment, mobilize or paralyse the processes of communication. In the relative effectiveness of communication lies the cryptic presence or absence of neurotic disturbance between the group in which the individual is lost or in which he is found (Gardner Murphy). The continuous dilemma or dialectic between the individual and group, at the interface between the irreconcilable pluralism and their 'plurel' or monism, creates tension and activates processes of communication. For this very reason the structure must be fostered and promoted continuously, as this is the source of activation within the group situation, of all groups in fact, and it is the degree of tension thus generated which can either mobilize or paralyse or fragment or unite, depending on the stage in development of the matrix.

Though there remains a great deal more to be understood about the question of number, the structure of the small psychotherapy group usually consists of seven to eight members, seated in a circle round a table, with the conductor as part of the circle, meeting for about an hour and a half, once or more a week, the discussion being a-programmatic and the conductor behaving relatively non-directively, as far as possible. He takes into account all that is going on and regards the discussion phenomenologically in the light of self-defining group association, which he regards descriptively and as far as possible 'without prejudice'. This can provide him with self-evident themes whose content can guide him to handle the situation therapeutically – and the more self-evident these themes become, the less he has to interpret, and the more information they provide.

The group structure is the most significant single contribution that group therapy has made to psychotherapy, its main features being that it is small, it is face-to-face, it meets regularly and it pursues a free-flowing discussion theme and there is no topic that must not be discussed (even if it so arises, the weather). Potentially, it is an intensely activating primary group, whose introduction marks a central discovery not only for psychotherapy, but for sociology, psychology and philosophy generally. It is no exaggeration to say that as a deliberate procedure, it is unique in the history of mankind. It starts off by being a disorganized plurality of autonomously functioning individuals, often hardly a group at all in the sense of being an entity, a 'serialization'. There is no *a priori* reason to assume it will, in fact, become a metastructural entity, and the therapist's role at this stage is active because he has, in fact, instituted matters. He has selected and invited the members, he has made arrangements and suggested an early procedure: also he is seen as active and powerful in representing the clinic in which he works. In this phase, the group is an a-historic social system, with the matrix at a rudimentary stage in communicational development. It has an immediate, primitively powerful impact, with a characteristic type of 'transpersonal' response rather like a transference but of which immediacy and transcience are characteristic features (which we shall go into more fully later), and which constitutes the prime mover 're-animating the archaic inheritance direct', 'a good match for the ancient super-ego' (Foulkes).

At this stage communication is mainly unspoken and is based on instinctual patterns of which identification is perhaps the most striking, directly with each other and complementarily with the conductor, for the members have been brought together by pressures outside themselves, by the clinic for instance, rather than by any personal involvements 'connecting individuals in a technically temporary organization, but not inwardly', as Karl Jaspers has put it, referring to larger groups. Intrapersonal communication at this phase (of which symptom formation and the recalled dream are examples), remains on the level of an intrapersonal monologue, and such communication as does occur is predominantly 'impersonally' transpersonal, and cliché-ridden, for instance identification, with such manifestations as symptom swopping, evoking feelings of a crude massive character, such as 'togetherness', in having neurosis in common and in sharing similar expectations in regard to therapy and therapist – identification as distinct from the introjectionary processes of learning.

It is perhaps at this stage, or of this sort of group that Bion comments, 'the idea neurotics cannot co-operate has to be modified', and he applies the slogan 'Vendors of quack nostrums unite!' – a group in which people are combined by a primitive 'tropism' or non-mental tie, which he terms 'valency'.

The group in this early phase is like larger groups which induce a sense of loss of personal identity or ego-feeling. The repressing forces are projected on to the leader, with which role in other groups he usually colludes; the group matrix is still only a makeshift, loose affair and emotions of devotion, hate, fear and rage, are expressed explosively, if expressed at all. In the larger group formations, a state prevails in which such phenomena as the flight response of panic can appear when the group fragments or, alternatively, these can be prevented by instituting regimes of rigidly disciplined organization analogous to reaction formations, to a hypnotic state, which Freud describes as a group of two. In the small group setting, similar episodes come into play in such manifestations as Foulkes's 'condenser reaction', which will be described later.

Freud pointed out that two sorts of tie exist in groups (at the interpersonal level), namely, first, that of regression to the earliest (intrapersonal) type of oral relationship (identification), when object-cathexis and identification are indistinguishable and which occurs between the members in relationship to each other; secondly, that of object-choice of the leader (but which also contains the projection of the individual's ego ideal and which would seem to relate to the later concept of projective identification). He therefore postulated two sorts of psychology apparent in group psychology, which he regarded as the oldest human psychology, namely that of the individual members of the group and that of the leader. He surmised there must be a possibility of transforming group psychology into individual psychology, 'a condition must be discovered under which such a transformation is easily accomplished, in which object choice advances from identification with one another'. I would say that it is in these bald terms that he clearly states the questions and, therefore, also the dilemma of the group setting. As far as group therapy is concerned, this is the crux of the whole matter, for if the small group situation could provide something akin to this 'condition', it would be this which would constitute the very essence of group psychotherapy.

To offset fragmentation, groups in these rudimentary stages of communication appear to form a pattern along the lines he describes, a pattern which also, incidentally, reconstitutes the intrapersonal level, the individual's inner world: 'a primary group of this kind is a number of individuals who have substituted one and the same object for their ego ideal and have consequently identified themselves with one another in their ego.'

At this point, then, what object relationship there is takes the form of the shared object choice of the therapist by the members. Because of the ties of identification, the group has a stereotyped, uniform quality which gave rise in the past to such concepts as McDougall's or Trotter's 'herd instinct' or Durkheim's 'group mind', a mind which differed in quality from that of the individual, and took on a distinctly arbitrary form. What was not sufficiently appreciated was that this represents a social system at a certain early stage in development in its history, and is by no means characteristic of all groups, a group with a still rudimentary system of communication.

Placed in this antithetically constituted environment, the individual is split by a dualism that is neither gratifying nor realistic, involving on the one hand a loss of personal identity with a crude, mass identification with the other members on the other, with an object choice of the conductor or leader as the case may be. This state of affairs can only be maintained by instituting external pressures which promote uniformity and authoritarianism as seen in large groups such as the Church or army, on which these earlier studies of group psychology were based.

Small group psychotherapy begins precisely at this point, the point at which Freud left off, for instead of maintaining this situation, it does the reverse, having established the group situation, it leaves matters to the members to take over. From the word go, the conductor starts up a gradual process of strategic withdrawal, taking care not to demand more than the group can manage, and the long haul of his own 'decrescendo' of decentralization, of the take-over by the group matrix, has begun. This move towards a take-over bid receives its impetus from the tension that the situation creates in the first place. The individual is activated to change, and this change implies a reversing of the processes already set in motion by the fact that no supporting structure has been volunteered by the conductor. It implies interaction and communication with each other which constitutes the participation of object-choice as well as identification. In so doing, the members elaborate their own network or matrix of communication which is more rewarding and more appropriate.

There would seem to be a significant but undefined relationship between the unconscious personal repressed, and the unconscious but unrepressed 'collective' or group unconscious that becomes activated in group situations. By the lifting of the repressing forces inside the individual, and their projection on to the conductor, the inner configuration of the personality becomes radically, if transiently, altered and this, it is postulated, can be harnessed to therapeutic purposes. That then is the essence of the problem – in what way to make use of these group specific processes which are intrinsic to all groups everywhere, for psychotherapeutic purposes.

We have already noted that Freud considered a neurosis in making a person asocial could be cured (he called it a distorted cure), in certain specific group situations. He added 'if he is left to himself, a neurotic is obliged to replace by his own symptom formations the great group formations from which he is excluded,' and 'thus recapitulate the institutions of humanity in a distorted way.' We shall later see that this bears relevance in relationship to the group matrix, for the latter undergoes a series of emerging and progressively more socialized patterns which become imprinted upon the locus; the latter then takes on various fantasy meta-structural meanings, depending on the pattern of the matrix at any one particular moment – for instance, a family circle, a stage, a forum, 'the community', a court of justice, a cabal. Essentially none of these things, it remains a suspended, transitional 'proxy' entity, quasi-fantasy, quasi-real, involving the ludic principle of play, equivalent to the analyst in the psychoanalytic situation.

With its a-programmatic procedure, it can be compared to a stage without script or a law court without a legal code, around which are woven the changing patterns (some relatively more stable than others), of a spontaneous psychodrama ranging from more hierarchical primitive, leader-centred structures to progressively more decentralized, more complex, and socialized forms (social is derived from a word meaning to share), in which the individual emerges as a true participant in social relationships, a true 'socius'. Matters are so arranged that the stage remains relatively encapsulated and protected. Relaxation of current social defences is encouraged, and this facilitates the testing-out of new roles. At the same time, its boundaries are not hermetically sealed, and have been compared with a semi-permeable membrane to an open system. However, as in psychoanalysis, resistance often takes the form of attempts to disrupt the mandatory framework of the situation by such ploys as late-coming, absenteeism, irregularity or meetings outside the situation, and it is one of the conductor's most important functions to interpret these occurrences as early as possible.

The locus can be compared to a sounding-board or stage. It both amplifies and offers opportunities for projecting and dramatizing neurotic trends by mobilizing role-playing. Individuals personify the threads that constitute the knotted conflict of a neurosis in other members. In the plays, Oedipus carries out each and all the partial impulses completely and totally – these, however, are splayed out serially – murder, incest, punishment, atonement and eventually a painless ascension into heaven – as opposed to being tangled up in the form of the knotted neurotic symptom. The group's performance at this stage has been described by Bion as devoid of intellectual content, and conversation appears more or less futile. It behaves as if it had taken for granted certain 'basic assumptions'. In his opinion, unless these (what he terms) psychotic areas are laid bare, no real therapy can result, for they contain as he sees it the ultimate sources of group behaviour. He compares the task of coping with the group with that of the baby and the breast. People react anonymously in ways that are unconscious. This he calls 'the group mentality', and if the individual behaves at variance with it, he feels disagreeably affected. The group mentality takes on the patterns of three 'basic assumptions', namely fight-flight (a paranoid type of reaction), dependency (depression and guilt characterize this pattern), or pairing (hope and expectancy prevail).

Bion describes the individual as a 'group animal at war', and one gains the impression that his descriptions are based on these early phases in a group's history. The more constructive and sophisticated constellation he calls the 'work group', of which, he says, the conductor is the natural leader, and which has characteristics similar to those attributed by Freud to the ego which, he comments, 'triumphs in the end'. He sees this work group as a construct more or less antithetical to the basic assumption groups, and supports McDougall's formulation that organization removes the psychological disadvantages of group formation, but he makes no reference to any process of group maturation as conceived by Foulkes in his concept of the group matrix. Much of what Bion describes would suggest artefactual phenomena, the outcome of an unevolved group organization, of people placed suddenly and unprepared in a situation of relative disorganization for which they are neither provided nor equipped to cope with, owing to the almost entire absence of a group matrix or any substitutive system of communication such as a declared task or topic.

The intrapersonal aspect also bears affiliations with the psychobiological descriptions of instinct theory of McDougall and the early Freudians. The individual is in a state of isolation – man versus civilization – and Freud saw the problem as being one of 'how to provide for the group precisely those features which were characteristic of the individual and which are extinguished in him by the formation of the group', which is a holistic, idealistic rendering of the group as a whole, a danger incidentally, which Aristotle had foreseen when he criticized Plato's Utopia on the grounds that it aimed too much at unity within the state, which would therefore be transformed into a sort of hyper-individual; on the contrary, he saw the very nature of a state to be a plurality of dissimilars, of diversity of functions. The attempts to procure for the group features characteristic of the individual presupposes the small group cannot become a teleological apparatus in its own right and cannot develop a metastructure, that it is incapable of displaying any functional autonomy or immanent teleology, and must therefore remain centred on the individual ego of the leader.

Most approaches in group therapy appear to fail to do justice to the inherent potentialities of the small group system itself, which is both monistic and pluralistic – 'a group of individuals'. This is not merely a theoretical play on words, for it influences our handling of the situation in promoting the greatest possible freedom for both individuals and group factors, otherwise there is no object in limiting the group to this particular number, both small enough and big enough for each participant to play his role to the full. The small therapeutic group, in fact, throws light on the age-old question of the relationship of the particular to the general – of the part to the whole. Within this framework and with a non-directive procedure and free-floating discussion, a meeting-place between the two constructs 'individual' and 'group', 'leader' and 'led' disappear, for it is their interaction that determines each other, and people discover freedom, but in a social setting.

An interesting but not unexpected observation of groups heavily loaded 'intrapersonally' is described in Freeman's, Cameron's and McGhie's book *Chronic Schizophrenia* (1958). It concerns a group of schizophrenic patients who met four times a week over a period of several months. 'As the months went by, in spite of much activity by the patients, we came to the conclusion that there was no evidence of group formation and that they were still behaving as a number of isolated individuals.' The problem would therefore seem to be not that the inner world is itself schizophrenic, as many writers have supposed (Jung), but rather that it is the problem of isolation that makes it so – the social rather than the personal split.

This brings us to the *second construct* [II], that of the *group process* of *interpersonal communicating*, of duologue, which had until recently been regarded as the preserve of all comprehensive forms of 'individual psychotherapy', and which becomes incalculably remodelled in the context of the group setting.

As has already been pointed out, psychotherapy had its beginnings in a monadic setting – the patient was studied in a state of Cartesian isolation from a transcendental idealistic viewpoint of the subject-object dichotomy of a body-mind duality, leading to the sterility of facultative, motorized psychology, to the Wundtian laboratory and the 14,000 instincts, to McDougall's psychology and instinct theory, and to behaviourism. It was in this physicalist context that Freud initiated his 'id' psychology of the eternal instincts, whose structure 'never changes'; but already in his *Studies of Hysteria* (1895), he was on to the decisive factor of the sexually motivated, transference phenomenon, which gave meaning to the hysterical symptoms and which, in the form of a fuller understanding of this two-person unit, opened a possible therapeutic solution. This was further elaborated with the advent of the counter-transference concept in 1910.

In other words, Freud rapidly moved from the psychobiological intrapersonal or monadic level of Kraepelian psychiatry to the dynamic, dyadic, interpersonal level, but he did not move on to the transpersonal in its own right. Later still (1934 onwards), certain analysts further developed the interpersonal as opposed to the intrapersonal (Ferenczi, Fairbairn, Klein, Strachey, Rickman, Bion and others), rigorously adhering only to 'here and now' transference interpretations, which could be tested out in the future, questioning only the incongruities of the relationship with the analyst in the immediate situation, regarding all other interpretations of the past or outside the analysis as contestable and unverifiable, and therefore as redundant. Similar emphasis as to the interpersonal relationship has been made by such writers as Harry Stack Sullivan, who gave primacy to the interpersonal field in the treatment of schizophrenics in particular, and by such psychotherapists as Professor Karl Rogers (who has since become interested in groups) in his counsellor-client centred therapy 'nondirective counselling', holding that the self under proper conditions is capable of reorganizing its perceptual field and thus of altering behaviour more coherently. As we have said, in group therapy this interpersonal level represents an inevitable step out of the tension-creating situation of the group structure, for people naturally turn to communicating and exchanging with each other, particularly as the therapist neither offers to lead nor provides any alternative occupation. In doing this, or rather in not doing this, a crucial step unique in the history of groups has been taken of invoking transpersonal functioning.

At first, intercommunication tends to relate to the therapist even though he does not encourage it. Not surprisingly to begin with, many psychoanalytically orientated group therapists give it particular attention – for instance, Wender, Schilder, Slavson, Wolf and Schwartz in the United States saw group analysis as nothing more than psychoanalysis of individuals in groups. Then in this country, Bion, Rickman, Ezriel and Sutherland developed a technique which approximated to some extent to treating the group as a whole, as if all its contributions were the product of one patient – really as if the group had a mind which they then proceeded to analyse. Bion has termed it the group mentality, and Ezriel describes something similar in his 'common group tension' which is the common denominator of the members' shared preoccupations. He proceeds, once this has shown itself, to analyse the role that each member adopts in relation to it, pointing out, on the one hand, the desired relationship and, on the other, the avoided relationship contingent upon the calamity that would ensue. In these approaches and in various ways the interpersonal level has been, if anything, overemphasized and has tended to distort the potentially more complex and delicate transpersonal processes which can, if permitted, emerge in groups.

For instance, Bion states, seemingly inconsistently, that he attaches 'no intrinsic importance to the coming together of the group. It is important that the group should come sufficiently close to me to be able to give an interpretation without having to shout it.' 'The apparent difference between group psychology and individual psychology is an illusion.' 'I agree with Freud's protest that too much significance is thereby attributed to number' (so much for the concept of the primary group), and he rejects the idea of a group being more than the sum of its members since it is unnecessary. He bases his approach on the two-level psychoanalytic model with the basic group mentality on the one hand, and its basic assumptions equivalent to the unconscious mind, which is the nearest he gets to a transpersonal concept, and the upper level of the 'work' or 'sophisticated' group of which the therapist is the natural leader on the other. He sums up by saying that 'Freud sees the group as a repetition of part-object relationships. It follows from this that the group would, in Freud's view, approximate to neurotic patterns of behaviour, whereas in my view they would approximate to the patterns of psychotic behaviour. The society or group that is healthy shows its resemblance to the family group as Freud describes it.' (*Experiences in Groups*, 1961). Similarly, Sutherland (1950) states: 'In our view this (reality testing) can only be done by the therapist pointing out to all members the unconscious content of the common tension and to each individual his particular defence against it, and his fears of the consequence if this unconscious aim were to be gratified.'

For Foulkes, Bion's basic group would be equivalent to a group setting in the early stages rather than later on, when it had had the opportunity of evolving a matrix, of going through a maturational process. This too is in contrast to Bion, who considers the psychotic patterns have to be uncovered (presumably at a later phase) if any real therapy is to result. For Foulkes the dilemma of the interface between individual and group emerges slowly into a group matrix of increasing complexity, of socialization and humanization.

Bion's inconsistency lay in his statement that it is the work group that triumphs in the long run and that if the psychiatrist can manage boldly to use the group instead of spending his time more or less apologizing for its presence, he will find that the numerous difficulties produced are more than neutralized by the advantages of a proper use of his medium. This is inconsistent in the sense that elsewhere he states that he attaches no importance to the 'coming together of the group' – virtually denying its presence therefore as an entity, except either as a psychotic phenomenon or as a rigidly structured work group with the analyst as its leader, which at best resembles the family group. Throughout his book, there is no hint or mention of a group *qua* group maturational process equivalent to Foulkes's construct of the group matrix and which is the *sine qua non* of the group analytic psychotherapeutic approach.

Some writers, such as Slavson (*A Textbook in Analytic Group Psychotherapy*, 1964) goes so far as to recommend the nipping in the bud of what he terms group dynamics or 'synergy' in therapeutic groups, since the therapeutic process, by its very nature, is antagonistic to group formation and group dynamics. By their very nature, he also adds, therapeutic groups favour interpersonal interaction rather than group patterns. He too gives the impression of referring only to the early pattern of a group system in which identification predominates and the 'group ego', as he puts it, is invested and personified by the leader.

Foulkes, in his postulation of the group matrix, differs essentially from these approaches. His aim is to enable the group to evolve into an apparatus that can treat itself. 'At the intrapersonal level the therapist refers part processes to the individual as a whole; in the two-person situation to the transference-counter-transference encounter as a whole, and in the group to the group as a whole, for psychoanalysis works on a psychoanalytic model and should not be transferred to the group, which operates on a group model with its transpersonal perspective and specific group features.'

The crucial modifications that occur in interpersonal communications in the group situations are:

(1) Intercommunications occur between patient and patient and not just between patient and therapist. There is, therefore, a situation in which patient treats patient on equal terms, based on a graduated feedback system of exchange, not on what is expected

but on what actually occurs, where teaching becomes a basis for learning.

(2) Communications, though interpersonal, are heard and therefore shared by all in the social situation, so that interpersonal communication takes place against a transpersonal background of the group matrix, in a context, therefore, which gives it not merely meaning for the two participants, but also a total meaning in relationship to the wider field of the group as a whole; we will go into this later. Suffice it to say here that, as an example, the development of a transference in this context has striking implications for the group in its repetitiveness and exclusiveness, and in its tendency to block other group processes, which therefore shows itself as a problem for the group as a whole.

(3) Intercommunication is part of a larger serial or 'chain reaction', an essential stepping-stone in a series of reactions, one triggering off the other, so that though it is not characteristic for the group situation, it is certainly crucial and gives rise to certain chains of events which constitute the basis for the next aspect, the transpersonal, which together with the group matrix, marks the group's most characteristic contribution.

Communication is built up, as we have said, through chains of interpersonal communication termed by Foulkes's 'group-association'. He is probably the first to have applied the term and it represents a decisive step in concept, for it profoundly affects the whole theory and method of application of group therapy, being specifically and primarily a group phenomenon. It modifies incalculably such concepts as the manifest, the latent, the repressed, and the unconscious, for here one has a situation in which the two units for study, namely the group and the individual, handle these matters differently – what is conscious to one individual may not be so to all and vice versa, what is repressed in one may be manifestly obvious to the others. It is precisely this transference of individual intrapersonal information and interpersonal communication into a transpersonal dialogue which constitutes the therapeutic potential of group therapy (though one would hardly gather this from much of the literature of the past, where only the therapist appears endowed with consciousness of what is 'really going on', which he 'analyses' and 'interprets').

The word 'consciousness' is derived from the Latin *conscius*, meaning knowing something with others. What is repressed in an individual is the outcome of personal experiences, so that themes unconscious to the individual participants develop in groups with a speed and clarity that one never sees in the dyadic situation – a theme for instance, that might take a year of daily analysis to emerge comes out in the course of a single (and even first) meeting. Where one member is blocked and another is not, the latter therefore is able to associate spontaneously without difficulty from where the previous member left off. These latent themes can be picked out like threads running through seemingly the most desultory conversations. Even if they are not spontaneously revealed or brought to the group's notice, at any rate they provide a fuller context which can guide the therapist. Group associations follow a centrifugal or centripetal course in relation to the theme, and the therapist is alive to their various detours and what they may indicate.

Where the chain reaction takes place less evenly, owing to strongly emotive processes being activated within an insufficiently evolved matrix, it may take the form of a series of jumps or an uneven pooling of only tenuously related associations (related however at a primary level), with an explosion of highly charged unexpected material. The term 'condenser phenomenon' has been applied to it. It represents a less articulate way of communicating where more articulate forms have yet to emerge. The rallying-point of Powdermaker and Frank, the basic assumptions of Bion and the common group tensions of Ezriel are related phenomena. In fact, many of the group phenomena that have been described are epiphenomena, being artefactual and arising from a techno-logical insufficiency in the communicational network.

As an outcome of transpersonal communication, the individuals composing the group are thrown into changing patterns of relation-ship, and the group is continuously being reconstructed into relatively more manifest constellations. Each communication reflects roles and traits that each is adopting in relation to the others. Role playing, therefore, is a central feature and the group develops a sort of physiognomy. The subject of role playing is a matter of its own and relates to personality and character disorders. Suffice it here to say that therapeutically speaking, role playing is one of the salient features of group therapy and enables the therapist to view these disorders in a living and meaningful context, for they are primarily socially determined. The word 'person' for instance, is derived from *persona* meaning 'mask through which sound comes' – in much the same way as 'role' is derived from the roll of manuscript containing the actor's script.

Freud, in his paper *Neurosis and Psychosis* (1924) wrote, 'It is always possible for the ego to avoid a rupture in any of its relations by deforming itself, submitting to forfeit something of its unity or, in the long run even to being gashed and rent, thus the illogicalities, eccentricities and follies of mankind now fall into a category similar to the sexual perversions, for by accepting them they spare themselves repressions.'

Sublimation, or the replacement of the instinctual aim in conformity with higher social values, appears only after repression has been lifted, and it would seem very readily and specifically to occur in the group situation, for instance social club therapy. It is related to identification, and the group situation therefore is one in which sublimation in the form of more apposite role emergence can readily be developed and remoulded. An interesting side effect of this factor in group therapy is mentioned by the Balints in *Psychotherapeutic Techniques in Medicine* (1961), in their remark to the effect that 'Perhaps one might be justified in saying that after a successful psychoanalytic treatment a patient is definitely less neurotic (or psychotic), but perhaps not necessarily really mature; on the other hand, after a successful treatment by group methods, the patient is not necessarily less neurotic, but inevitably more mature.'

The development and change of role playing in relation to the prevailing code of the group matrix which has been created by the members themselves is a crucial feature of a group therapy, but is easily overlooked, as roles may parade as 'normal' and therefore pass unquestioned behind invisible barriers of 'normality' and conformity. Members may maintain with considerable determination a barrage of circumstantial evidence, not because they are in the least concerned with the content of what they are saying, but because of the light in which these disclosures place them or because this role prevents another from emerging.

Referring back to [III] – what then constitutes the group content or matrix? Briefly, it is the total transpersonal network of communication that becomes laid down by the interactions of the previous two in their communication with each other. Communication in this context is regarded as all the events occurring in this situation which can be observed. As a concept, the matrix is of central importance for, given the opportunity, it can become an orderly self-emergent metastructure cemented by intersubjective intrapsychic meaning, offering us a pure group phenomenology. It provides the full context and background that is so characteristic of any comprehensive group work. The group structure, to begin with, starts up as an anonymous, often rather frightening, unknown 'serialization' of people chosen in series. It differs as a system from the previous category of interpersonal communication in that the latter figures in the relatively 'here and now' perspective as a foreground phenomenon.

In so far as it contains the past events of what has been communicated of the group's history, it has extensions into their past, but also it refers to present and future events, for it shapes and is shaped by past, present and future events. It is a social microcosm, forming a changing backcloth to the foreground figures of the other categories of the triad. It could be compared with the reversed order of a stage production, where the backcloth (the matrix), determines the stage (the structure), and the stage determines the script (the process). It is a continuously changing phenomenon which, it is pointed out, should not be anchored to any particular perspective in time or space. It should not be confined to the institution or the society or community outside the group, or to the group as a whole itself, or to any particular individual or individuals or to the conductor, but should be permitted to permeate all dimensions unobstructedly, phenomenologically. Neither the 'here and now' nor the 'there and then' can legitimately claim priority, for both are motivated continuously and simultaneously; both are continuously elaborated as the members continue to meet.

Although of itself it is only a network of channels of what has been communicated, it becomes invested with various and changing shapes or metastructures mapped out by the individuals who comprise it, who therefore play together and invest the group structure with various fantasy meanings, such as family, class, cabal, seminar, forum, playground or stage, community, society, humanity, reality.

In parenthesis, we have already noted that Sartre, in his *Critique of Dialectical Reason* (1960), considers groups in terms of organization, process, structure and function and, along lines similar to those presented here, has described 'group organization as defining its structure'. His reference to function provides a further aspect of the group which in this context would refer to its potential therapeutic purpose. These five aspects could be equated with the pre-philosophical notions of chaos, logos, cosmos, ethos and telos.

The group matrix begins, then, at the group's inception, steadily increases throughout and finishes at its termination for, as the processes of communicability and communicating continue, what has been communicated lays down a progressively more complex network or matrix or interface which takes on emerging meanings, a totalizing and synthesizing process with varying meanings, with a history, manifesting culture and codes influencing attitudes and roles. Most important is the fact that it can undergo a socializing or maturational and humanizing progression, even though this progression may have to proceed through many and extremely devious detours.

Foulkes puts it that 'in this group network all processes take place and in it they can be defined with regard to their meaning, their extension in time and space and their intensity', 'the operational basis of all mental processes in the group'. Their definition within the network of the group matrix has been called location, and it was this delineation of events within the group matrix of foreground figures of the group process of communicating against the background of the matrix (of what has been communicated), that marks the essential difference between his approach and all others, of which in 1948 he wrote: 'This type of observation represents another set of experiences which made me become a group analyst, because it provides a wider field in a fuller context than psychoanalysis for locating a dynamic system.' It is this which gives the group situation a living, four-dimensional quality.

Whilst in psychoanalysis the transference encounter is the cornerstone of treatment, in the group it is this process of locating that is primary, and if one were to pick out the essential features of Foulkes's approach contrasted with all others, it would be over this matter of location. It is a process which, though it has a tendency to emerge spontaneously, can be helped to do so by the therapist towards increasingly more articulate expression and is synonymous with therapy itself. It is only possible in the group setting, and places entirely different and fuller complexions on events, as distinct from those portrayed in the dyadic or monadic settings, for instance transference. 'Relatedness seen as taking place within a basic all-embracing group matrix is the cornerstone of our working theory.' It is a concept that is central and unique to Foulkes's approach, 'a new element under discussion', second only in importance to the small group setting itself, and it is 'at the centre of all our thinking about communication in groups'.

To review, then, the non-transference elements in group analytic psychotherapy, we remind ourselves that in his *Group Psychology and the Analysis of the Ego*, Freud wrote that 'from the first there were two kinds of psychology, that of the individual members of the group, and that of the father, chief or leader'.

He pointed out in the chapter headed 'A differentiating grade in the ego' that in the group setting, the individual gives up his ego ideal and substitutes for it the group ideal as embodied in the leader. The *'libidinal structure of the group leads back to the distinction between the ego and the ego ideal and to the double kind of tie which this makes possible – identification and the substitution of the object for the ego ideal.'*

He made comparison between hypnosis, being in love and the group psychology; he described hypnosis as a group of two.

He put it that a primary group 'is a number of individuals who have substituted one and the same object for the ego ideal and have consequently identified themselves with one another in their ego.' In other words, the repressive agent, namely the super-ego, becomes projected into the conductor *in a group setting* – and a corresponding intrapsychic change occurs within the individual, namely, a relatively less repressed ego structure.

Group therapy began at the point where Freud left off. Freud's philosophical background was based on the Cartesian dichotomy of the pure cogito, soul, spirit or *mind* (in this instance the psychoanalyst) observing *matter* (the patient); two totally distinct substances. (It is worth recalling, however, that Descartes did concede language as providing evidence of thought.)

The 'first scientific revolution' of Descartes and Newton liberated physics from the dead hand of the Scholastics, from anthropomorphism, but it took three centuries before the intangible data of the submicroscopic world, of psychology and sociology, could be accommodated by a new model in the philosophy of science and which has been nicknamed the second scientific revolution.

It has already been pointed out that Freud had to rely on the then current formulations in physics and science of philosophy at the beginning of the century, of the conservation of energy, of the intrapsychic world in isolation, of linear, unidirectional and progressive cause-effect relations, of psychic energy and economy.

Lewin, with the new models of quantum physics and electromagnetic field theory to draw from, where relationship and organization rather than energy and matter played a primary role, studied the intersubjective field. Round about 1939 he coined the terms group dynamics, systems in tension and field theory.

As has already been noted, with the advent of Wiener's and Shannon's cybernetics and information theory after World War II, the shift from the transference of energy to that of information, was finally established. With the discovery of feedback, of goal-directed behaviour in machines (such as the thermostat), the age-long epistemological controversy between determinism and teleology or vitalism (till then excluded from science) showed signs of a reconciliation. The crucial distinction between the psychodynamic (e.g. psychoanalytic) model on the one hand and the interdependence and interaction of the individual organism and the environment on the other, has been to some extent bridged by information and communication theory. Don Jackson in *Pragmatics of Human Communication* (1968) gives as an example the man who kicks a pebble; the latter will be displaced according to the amount of energy transferred: on the other hand, kicking a dog may result in a bite, when it is information rather than energy that is transferred. This is essentially the difference between Freudian psychodynamics and the theory of communication as explanatory principles of human behaviour, and which is so striking a feature of group dynamics.

Foulkes, inspired by Trigant Burrow in the first place, put the group in the centre of his orientation. 'That was and remains his great merit,' he said, speaking of Burrow.

Group psychotherapy, Foulkes stated (1964), can be practised with or without an analytic orientation; he himself is particularly concerned with the latter. In his early article of 1942, he states that the 'group has however, some specific therapeutic factors', of which he singles out (i) the sharing, socializing effect, (ii) the mirror reaction, (iii) the activating of the collective unconscious, the stimulating effect of the group situation, (iv) the exchange and information elements, (v) the form that communication took, namely that of group association modelled on free association, of free-floating discussion developed to its full extent. Essentially these group specific features which he elaborated upon later concern activation, communication and socialization of which socialization is specific to the group situation. 'This proves large enough (seven or eight patients and the therapist) to observe psychological reactions in their social context. The group is also large enough to be representative of its community, yet it is intimate enough to trace the ramifications of these reactions in the individual member and to explore their roots inside an individual.' (1949).

The group situation, in other words, 'introduces new features of its own which are not present in the individual situation between one therapist and one patient'. He said '*This is true though the majority of group therapists are not aware of it at the present time*' (1945). He sees the conductor's function as catalytic – as a participant observer – even though the group may attempt to put him into the position of a primordial leader.

'He can actually be said to be a father figure, and it is all too easy to interpret his position really as that of a father, a mother, and see the group as representing a family. *This is not my impression*' (1949). 'Group psychology must develop its own concepts in its own right and not borrow them from individual psychology. The group is older than the individual.'

Quoting Freud, 'we must conclude that the psychology of the group is the oldest human psychology'. The group, Foulkes suggests, reanimates the archaic inheritance, and it is the impetus of this reanimation which is harnessed for therapeutic purpose in group therapy.

The passing episodes of leadership (as described by Fritz Redl) in a continuous flow with a gradual decrescendo from his authoritarian position, are gradually replaced by reliance on the strength of the group itself, which Foulkes later developed in his theory of the group matrix. Two moves are taking place – a decrescendo away from authoritarianism and a crescendo towards socialization. Foulkes writes:

'*If he thinks for instance in terms of transference of the family group containing father, mother and siblings, of projection, identification, repression, resistance, reaction formation, fixation* and on merely in the way these appear in the individual situation he will find all these to be sure, in operation, *but he will not learn much that is new.* If he thinks, however, of the group situation which he has in front of him, he will find a wealth of new observations, as regards the *dynamics of the group* and indeed new light will be thrown upon the mechanisms operating in individual psychoanalysis.

'The paramount need here is to create a scientific view of group psycho-dynamics . . . in a language that is commonly understood . . . the group situation becomes the natural meeting-ground of the biologist, anthropologist, sociologist and psychoanalyst.

'We do not think that there are any such factors which may not appear in some guise in other types of group. What distinguishes our analytic groups is not the presence of certain unique factors but the particular combination of the several factors which we have already enumerated and the way in which they are used.

'There is the free-floating verbal communication carried to an extreme point; there is the maximum reduction of censorship of personal and interpersonal feelings; there is the attitude of the conductor, who not only actively cultivates and maintains the group atmosphere and the active participation of members, but also allows himself to become a transference figure in the psycho-analytic sense and accepts the changing roles which the group assigns him; there is the emphasis on the unconscious repressed of psychoanalysis and on the interpersonal and social unconscious in the group-analytic sense; there is analysis and interpretation of the material produced by the group.

'It is the concerted application of all these elements in a judic-iously selected interplay which makes a situation therapeutic. The *psychoanalytic situation is known in such a capacity as a "transference situation"*. Some writers (such as Ezriel) declare the group thera-peutic situation to be not more and not less than a transference situation in a group setting. As we have pointed out in the first chapter, we feel it *important to distinguish between transference and non-transference elements*, both being part of the therapeutic process. Therefore we propose to signify those properties of the (psycho-) therapeutic situation which makes it essentially therapeutic by the symbol "T". We can then formulate that some authors consider "T" as identical with "transference" (T=t), whereas the present authors consider that a "T" situation must allow for the dynamic confrontation of the patient with both the transference (t) and non-transference x=current relationships "here-and-now", etc.) aspects of his reactions. (T=t+x).

'In the T-situation past and present must meet. The past – which was unconscious, repressed or never experienced in such form as could be recalled except through repetition behaviour – is accepted as present in the T-situation. In the same process, however, the real present (the current situation, the immediate context, the "here-and-now") must be represented as well for the analytic therapeutic process to operate.

'In this connection, it is one of the relevant conditions that the participants in a group-analytic group are strangers except for their contact within the group. The very personal and real emotions and attitudes between members thus remain inside the T-situation, are prevented from spilling over into ordinary life.'

The transference situation in the group is on a much broader front – it is horizontal rather than vertical. The individual patient's transference relationship to the conductor or to any other member of the group cannot develop to anything like the same extent as in psychoanalysis and cannot always be analysed vertically to anything like the same degree.

'For the study of this wider field, of the location and constellation of his disturbance with its complex network of human relationship the group situation provides an indispensable means of bringing essential patterns into focus. Within the group analytic situation we have, instead of the individual transference relationship between patient and therapist, a whole spectrum of relationship in active operation before our eyes.'

Foulkes points out that whilst in psychoanalysis the interpretations are made by the analyst, *in the group all members participate actively*. It is a multipersonal situation in which regression, includ-ing the strictly psychoanalytic phenomenon of transference, is not encouraged. The full analysis of individual transference is not possible and the transference neurosis is not fully promoted and established. Whilst in psychoanalysis there is verbal analysis with emphasis on insight and on contact between past and present – in group analysis the emphasis is upon action and experience – ego training in an active and a corrective experience, not by the analyst but by the slowly emerging group network which becomes pro-gressively more complex and sophisticated and affiliative as distinct from hierarchical.

In brief, the group situation has an immediate and very powerful impact – if you wish to, you can call it a sort of collective archaic transference which is universal, for it occurs in all groups every-where and is not confined to neurotics (as transference is said to do in the transference neurosis), nor is it unconscious. In fact, the projecting of the ego ideal on to the conductor or leader results in a lifting of repressive forces within the individual. The content of the personal repressed is not the focus of interest – rather a pro-found modification takes place in the super-ego once it becomes, as it were, the property of the group, which is then translated from a primitive archaic authoritarian institution by communication whether intrapersonal, interpersonal or transpersonal, and is treated in whatever form it arises. This therefore does not exclude transference interpretations, provided this is forming the greater barrier but the effect of such interpretation may have its repercussions in rendering the group constellation more leader-centred.

Bion put it succinctly that 'in the treatment of the individual, neurosis is displayed as a problem of the individual. In the treatment of a group, it must be displayed as a problem of the group.'

All approaches can be expressed diagrammatically and located in relationship to each other within a triangular area depending upon such variables as task, members, orientation of conductor, size of group. The positionings of the various approaches are only approximations, serving as indications or suggestions.

See diagram:

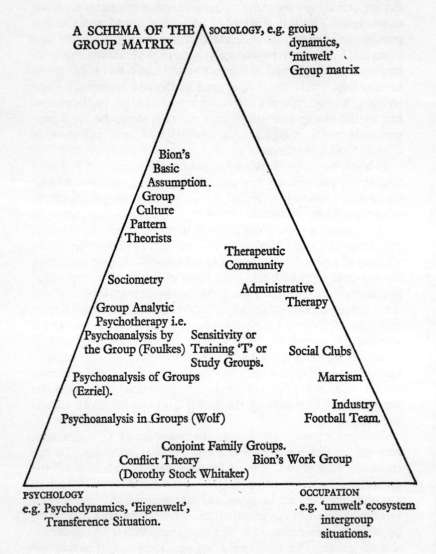

A SCHEMA OF THE GROUP MATRIX

SOCIOLOGY, e.g. group dynamics, 'mitwelt' Group matrix

Bion's Basic Assumption. Group Culture Pattern Theorists

Therapeutic Community

Sociometry

Administrative Therapy

Group Analytic Psychotherapy i.e. Psychoanalysis by the Group (Foulkes)

Sensitivity or Training 'T' or Study Groups.

Social Clubs

Psychoanalysis of Groups (Ezriel).

Marxism

Psychoanalysis in Groups (Wolf)

Industry Football Team.

Conjoint Family Groups.
Conflict Theory   Bion's Work Group
(Dorothy Stock Whitaker)

PSYCHOLOGY
e.g. Psychodynamics, 'Eigenwelt',
Transference Situation.

OCCUPATION
e.g. 'umwelt' ecosystem
intergroup
situations.

To summarize then – individuals, as a result of finding them-selves in the paradoxical setting of the group structure in its early stages, are captive, or subjected, as we have said, to a dialectical process, to a dichotomy and splitting that is neither appropriate nor gratifying – therefore, to communicate and to share, and in so doing to elaborate the matrix, the network of what has been communicated, which is both more realistic and more rewarding, and though still a dualism, is no longer dichotomous. Also, in so doing, they are not being indoctrinated or, if so, then it is by their own doctrines. This is an extension of the Lewinian finding that change in individuals is facilitated in group situations, or of Sherif's finding also – that membership in a group affects per-ception. Foulkes has compared the group matrix to the network of association fibres in the brain – the operational basis of all mental processes in the group.

The relationship of the conductor to the matrix is important for, as the matrix grows, the role of the conductor tends to recede. In the early stages, when he is at the focus of the group's attention, he is relatively at his most active – indeed in instituting the group in the first place he has been very active, even though it has been from behind the scenes.

In the communicational processes, he attempts to move along-side them, neither dragging nor having to be dragged, but 'catalys-ing' matters by judicious interpretations, particularly of resistances which seem to be holding up the group processes. In the con-figurations of the matrix he plays a relatively passive role, allowing himself to be manœuvred, but not fixed into any particular posi-tion. The process tends to be cyclical. The final configuration of the matrix is imprinted upon the structure which, in becoming a metastructure, initiates a new cycle, beginning again intraperson-ally. This steady take-over from the initial authorisation/chaos dichotomy by a progressively evolving matrix which permeates intrapersonal as well as intragroup (transpersonal) dimensions, represents an essential feature in the therapeutic process.

The dilemma for the conductor is that he tends either to collude with, or rebut his assigned position, that he freezes and fixates or, alternatively crushes the ongoing configurations at any one particular phase, particularly those at which group communication is both rudimentary and compelling.

To summarize – the group matrix relates in at least four main directions, namely:

(a) To the conductor.
(b) To the group structure.
(c) To the three perspectives of communication, (intra-, inter-, and transpersonal), future, present, and past.
(d) And to the community at large – outside group.

(a) In relationship to the conductor, there is a total push from the split of the initial stages of members identifying with each other in a leader-centred constellation, to the progressively evolving matrix of the final stages, which permeates intra-, inter-, and transpersonal levels, and enables the members both individually and as a whole to take over their own leadership function, a social solution to the family Oedipal conflict.

(b) In relation to the structure, there is the continually changing play of emerging patterns which guide the therapist and which imprint themselves or configurate the structure, weaving patterns of fantasy meanings ranging from the mechanical and archaic to more sophisticated forms, for instance, the horde, the family, the gang, the court of justice, stage, forum, the game, the social microcosm, the playground. The matrix then lies in an antithetical position to the plurality existing within the group structure itself, and confers upon it these evolving metastructures, if given the opportunity.

(c) In relation to the three perspectives of communication, the matrix forms the background against which the foreground communications between the group members are highlighted and located.

(d) Finally, in relation to the community at large, the unique contribution of the matrix lies in the introduction of a manœuvrable social dimension into the actual fabric of the technique itself, so that it forms a gateway through which the isolated individual can rediscover his 'socius' and retrace a social dimension – shedding the configurations of his own isolating super-ego, alternatively revising the boundaries of his either too compliant conformism or the psychopathic defections of a personality disorder. The social situation of the group, however, by contrast brings out real guilt (social responsibility) and valid anxieties in a manner that is overlooked in other settings, for instance in the isolation of the dyadic relationship or in the massive impersonal alienation of the large secondary group structures of today, for a person feels no responsibility in a situation where he is lonely. The problem is not one of intimacy between individuals, but of intimacy between individuals in a social setting.

The matrix, in becoming social (secondary socialization), as opposed to family-constellated (primary socialization), is guilt-free, and the conductor is seen in his socially valid role. This is reflected intrapersonally when the super-ego becomes accordingly modified to function ego-syntonically as an ego-ideal, both socialized and humanized.

Whittaker and Lieberman have said something similar in their book, *Psychotherapy through the Group Process* (1964). They state: 'The development of the therapy group from its inception to its termination is characterized by a recurrence of basic themes under progressively expanding cultural conditions.'

Let me quote an example. Mr Voyeur severely castigates another member, Mr Photographer, who takes photographs of nudes in his spare time. V feels P should be making better use of a university degree which P has acquired and which V very much envies, as he himself has never been able to concentrate. The other members pick up and locate V's censorious attitude towards P. They place this in the foreground and P's voyeurism in the background. The conductor is a little surprised at this course of events because the group to date has tended towards prudishness, and a leader- or family-centred configuration; but he is guided by what is quite clearly the group members' location of the problem. Also, he is aware, which the other members are not, that V suffers from compulsive voyeurism which, on occasion, has involved him with the police; it is only after the severity of V's attitude has been located, questioned, and discussed by the group that he reveals his own problem in that direction.

In this example, then, two members have a problem in common which one confesses and the other condemns. It is left to the shared but more recent attitude of the metastructure which has been emerging in the course of the development of the matrix in the background, to locate the problem as one of inappropriate harshness, which can neither be finally located intrapersonally, in one or other member, nor just interpersonally, but must also be viewed transpersonally, involving the group as a whole (the group matrix), and even in the last resort, the community as a whole (the social matrix), in the form of the police. A complexity of all three aspects is involved against the background of the group matrix, and even the outside social matrix is called into question. The group as a whole, in deciding to take up their own line of enquiry, instead of looking to the therapist or to the community for arbitration and in being less censorious, are manifesting a new departure in the metastructure or configuration of their matrix, so that it changes its fantasy meaning from that of a family (often with a highly intransigent father and mother and sibling figures), to that of a social group, representing one of the primary 'morphogenic' steps in any small group which purports to be therapeutic, and in which intimacies can be openly discussed without anxiety or symptomatic disguise.

Schematically speaking therefore, it might be possible (indeed in my opinion it should be possible), in all closed groups to decipher a progression of group constellations ranging through an initial phase of archaic subhuman and mechanical manifestations, which might be analogous to the pre-genital phases of infantile development, in the same way as the comparison made by Bion of the group to the infantile efforts to contend with relating to the breast ('psychotic mechanisms'). The metastructure in such instances takes on the form of identification and projection, for example, leader-centred and needlessly authoritarian. The group then proceeds, given the opportunity, to a family constellation – not as Bion suggests as a manifestation of health – but as a stage on the way to achieving its potential and potent function as a social network which has yet to be defined, but has the sort of qualities of Bion's work group and is a communicational nexus in which informational flow occurs to the extent that cannot be in groups where 'transference', coercion, hierarchy, and 'energy flow' remain paramount.

Many groups, perhaps most, do not go beyond this family constellation – typically various members take on parental or sibling roles which they may be unwilling to relinquish and which do not by any means always revolve around the therapist. Clashes over these roles may be expressed without insight by forceful aggression directed against change. Members may leave at this stage having improved, but fundamental sexual problems remain unsolved. However, these may have been rendered less intransigent by these rehearsals of old family scores. I think probably most slow-open groups remain at this level.

The third or final stage seems to me to be one where the delicate fabric of gentle thought processes and communication can emerge more freely and with fuller insight – where both the individual participants and the group as a whole can discover for the first time the true meaning of social expansion and legitimate power. Members both play upon and are played upon by the group, and thoughts and words and ideas are inspired in a manner that cannot occur in any other situation.

The group analytic situation is one in which a manœuvrable social dimension in the form of the group matrix can be manipulated for therapeutic, that is, for both socializing and humanizing purposes. It is manœuvrable in the sense that it is elaborated by the members themselves, and it is manipulated by the therapist in such a way as to enable the projected super-ego to undergo a maturational development beginning with mechanical, archaic forms, and progressing to a more human and socially appropriate one, one that is ego-syntonic. In Anthony's words, 'the socializing effect, the therapeutic effect, and the communication effect run hand in hand and it is difficult to separate them', for the group situation can mobilize the institutions of the id, activate the ego, and above all, modify the super-ego.

This is vital, for in the last resort not merely the outcome of a neurosis but the fate of our entire civilization must depend on a capacity to rise to 'One-ness', to achieve fellowship or koinonia as the Greeks termed it.

What does the future hold? I think it is likely to be concerned not only with small and medium-sized groups, not only with controversy over therapeutic community and community therapy, but with much larger psychotherapeutic groups with a membership of fifty to a hundred, conducted by several co-conductors; non-directive and a-programmatic with tiered circular seating arrangements reminiscent of the amphitheatre. In this situation group dynamics become extremely clearly defined and atmospheres, attitudes, ideas, and ideologies make themselves evident not as cloudy, idealistic, non-sequiturs but as definitive climates which can be seen as either impeding, coercing or promoting communication, and which are themselves the objects of study. In these larger groups is more clearly seen the antithesis, the polarization of conscious and unconscious. The problem for the individual is the intrusion in the individual situation of the repressed unconscious. For the large group on the other hand, it is consciousness that is in jeopardy, both for the individual and for the group's equivalent of consciousness, namely communication and organization. The problem for the rudimentary large group is its mindlessness.

Neurosis and certain of the psychoses are as localized little worlds or deposits of unresolved group experience in the individual's past, or present, or even future situations. It is this which renders the traumatic neuroses understandable in group terms, for they are not explicable in terms of the infantile neuroses.

Individuals brought up in restrictive atmospheres which block communication may suffer from the implosive effect of such a backward thrust which manifests itself therefore intrapersonally, either psychologically (as in drug addiction) or somatically similar to the 'proto-mental' system construed by Bion, in which epidemics, economic or psychosomatic crises are produced rendering creative impulses destructive.

People in groups create group climates consisting of unconscious, rejected fantasies and parts of themselves which are projected, and produce atmospheres which are, as I have said, neither realistic nor gratifying. This they then have to work through in various stages or cultures. For example, an anxious person has to persuade his group to produce a frightening feeling, a paranoid has to produce actual persecution before he has the opportunity to work, indeed to fight his way through what really now is in the group and is therefore no longer delusional. In other non-therapeutic situations he either runs away or is forced out before he can solve it, and therefore keeps repeating the experience rather than resolving it. For this the term *transposition* rather than transference would seem more appropriate.

In the introduction I started off by alluding to a map. At the risk of being accused of reification I should like to end by offering such a chart which can act as a guide through the multiplicity of group variables. I hope it is to some extent self-explanatory and will shed light on the primary nature of panic and rage which are at the core of most psychological and group disturbances. Source and social selves are polarized as two views of the authentic self, both of which need to be brought continuously into relationship with each other. When they become split primary, uncontainable, incommunicable, and unusable panic or aggression ensue; when they relate however there is an awareness of meaning and a consciousness of self, a self that can wish and choose what sort of self to be, a 'knowing something in oneself with others'. (*Shorter Oxford Dictionary*'s derivation of consciousness).

(See diagram overleaf.)

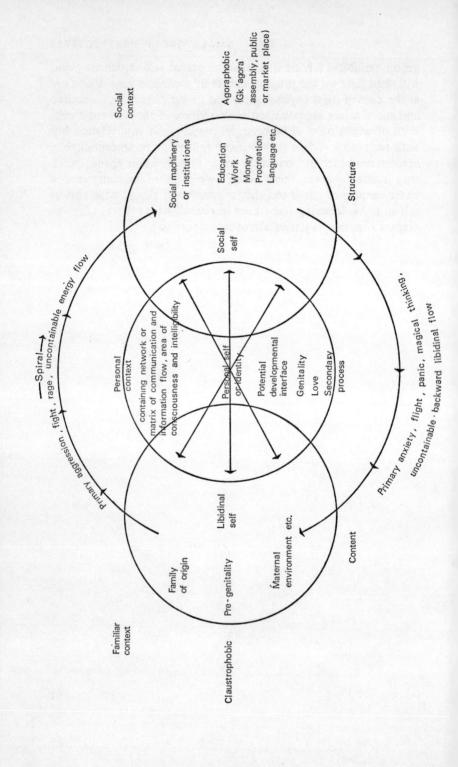

Bibliography

ABERCROMBIE, J. M. L., *The Anatomy of Judgement* (Hutchinson, 1960).
      'Group Methods in Education'. Monograph by the Society for Research in Higher Education, 1969.

ALLPORT, G. W., *Personality. A Psychological Interpretation* (Holt, New York, 1937).
      Personality and Social Encounter (Boston, Beacon Press, 1960:1964).

ARGYLE, M., *The Psychology of Interpersonal Behaviour* (Penguin, London, 1967).

BACH, G. R., *Intensive Group Therapy* (Ronald Press, New York, 1954).

BAIR, L. (trans.), *Essential Works of Descartes* (Bantam Books, New York, 1961).

BALINT, M. and E., *Psychotherapeutic Techniques in Medicine* (Tavistock, London, 1961).

BERGER, P. L. and LUCKMANN, T., *The Social Construction of Reality* (Allen Lane, The Penguin Press, London, 1967).

BERNE, E., *Transactional Analysis in Psychotherapy* (Grove Press, New York; Evergreen, London, 1961).

BERNSTEIN, B., *Language in Culture and Society*, Ed. D. Hynes (Harper & Row, New York, 1966).

BION, W. R., *Experiences in Groups* (Tavistock Publications, London, 1961).

BIRNEY, R. C. and TEEVAN, R. C. (eds.), *Instinct* (Van Nostrand, Princeton, 1961).

BRADFORD, L. P., GIBB, J. R. and BENNE, K. D. (eds.), *T-Group Theory and Laboratory Method* (John Wiley & Sons Inc, 1964).

BREISACH, E., *Introduction to Modern Existentialism* (Grove Press, New York, 1962).

BROWN, J. A. C., *The Social Psychology of Industry* (Penguin, London, 1954: 1963).
      Freud and the Post-Freudians (Penguin, London, 1961).

N

BUCKLEY, WALTER, *Sociology and Modern Systems Theory* (Prentice-Hall Inc., 1967).

BURROW, T., *The Neurosis of Man. An Introduction to a Science of Human Behaviour* (Routledge & Kegan Paul, London, 1949).

CAPLAN, G., *Principles of Preventive Psychiatry* (Tavistock, London, 1964).

CARTWRIGHT, D. and ZANDER, A. (eds.), *Group Dynamics. Research & Theory* (Tavistock, London, 1953:1960).

CASSIRER, E., *Substance and Function, and Einstein's Theory of Relativity)*, trans. W. C. and M. C. Swabey (Dover, New York, 1923:1953).
The Logic of the Humanities, trans. C. S. Howe (Yale U.P., New Haven and London, 1968).

CHISHOLM, R. M. (ed.), *Realism and the Background of Phenomenology* (Allen & Unwin, London, 1960).

CHOMSKY, N., *American Power and the New Mandarins* (Penguin, and Chatto and Windus, London, 1969).
Language and Mind (Harcourt, Brace, New York, 1968).

CLARK, A. W. and YOEMANS, N., *'Fraser House'* (Springer Publishing Co., Inc., N.Y., 1969).

CLARK, D., *Administrative Therapy* (Tavistock, London, 1964).

COLLINS, J., *The Existentialists. A Critical Study* (Regnery, Chicago, 1952:1963).

CORNFORD, F. M., *Before and After Socrates* (C.U.P., Cambridge, 1932:1964).
From Religion to Philosophy (Harper & Row, New York and Evanston, 1912:1957).

CORSINI, R. J., *Methods of Group Psychotherapy* (McGraw-Hill, 1957).

CRISP, A. H., *Therapeutic Aspects of the Doctor/Patient Relationship* (*Psychother. Psychosom.* 18: 12–33 1970).

DANIEL, G. R. and FREEMAN, H. L. (eds.), *The Treatment of Mental Disorders in the Community*. The Proceedings of a Symposium held in London . . . (1967) (Baillière, Tindall & Cassell, London).

DAVIES, J. T., *The Scientific Approach* (Academic Press, London and New York, 1965).

DE MARÉ, P. B., *'Some Theoretical Concepts in Group-Analytic Psychotherapy'*, International Handbook of Group Psychotherapy (Philosophical Library Inc., 1966).

DENBER, H. C. B. (ed.), *Research Conference on the Therapeutic Community Held at Manhattan State Hospital, Ward's Island, New York*, (Charles C. Thomas, Springfield, 1960).

DESAN, W., *The Marxism of Jean-Paul Sartre* (Doubleday, New York: Anchor Books, 1965:1966).

DEUTSCH, M., 'Field Theory in Social Psychology' in *Handbook of Social Psychology*, ed. G. Lindzey (Addison-Wesley, Reading, Mass. and London, 1954:1959).

DICKS, H. U., *Marital Tensions* (Routledge & Kegan Paul, London, 1967).

DOUGLAS, C. H., *The Monopoly of Credit* (C.R.P. Publications).

DRAKE, H. L. (abridged by), *Plato's Complete Works* (Littlefield, Adams, Patterson, N.J., 1959).

DURKHEIM, E., *Robert Bierstedt*, (Weidenfeld and Nicholson, 1966).

DUVERGER, M., *Introduction to the Social Sciences*, trans. M. Anderson (George Allen & Unwin, London, 1959:1961:1964). (Orig.: *Méthodes des Sciences Sociales*, Paris 1959).

DURKIN, H. E., *The Group in Depth* (International Universities Press, New York, 1964).

EDELSON, M., *Sociotherapy and Psychotherapy* (University of Chicago Press, 1970).

EMERY, F. E., (Editor), *Systems Thinking. Selected Readings* (Penguin Modern Management Readings, 1969).

EZRIEL, H., 'A Psychoanalytic Approach to Group Treatment', *British Journal of Medical Psychology*, Vol. XXIII, Parts 1 and 2, 1950).

FAIRBAIRN, W. R. D., *Psychoanalytic Studies of the Personality* (Tavistock, London, 1952).

FEYNMAN, R., *The Character of Physical Law* (B.B.C., London, 1965).

FOSS, B. M. (ed.), *New Horizons in Psychology* (Penguin, London, 1966)

FOULKES, S. H., *Introduction to Group-Analytic Psychotherapy* (Heinemann, 1948).

     Therapeutic Group Analysis (Allen & Unwin, London, 1964).

FOULKES, S. H. and ANTHONY, E. J., *Group Psychotherapy. The Psychoanalytic Approach* (Penguin, London, 1957).

FOULKES, S. H. and PRINCE, G. S. (eds.), *Psychiatry in a Changing Society* (Tavistock, London, 1969).

FRANKFORT, H. and H. A., WILSON, J. A. and JACOBSEN, T., *Before Philosophy. The Intellectual Adventure of Ancient Man* (Penguin, London, 1949. Orig.: *The Intellectual Adventure of Ancient Man*, Chicago, 1946).

FREEMAN, T., CAMERON, J. L. and McGHIE, A., *Chronic Schizophrenia* (Tavistock, London, 1958).

FREUD, SIGMUND, *Group Psychology and the Analysis of the Ego* (Hogarth Press, 1945).

     Totem and Taboo (Penguin, London, 1938. Orig.: *Totem und Tabu*, 1919).

FREUND, J., *The Sociology of Max Weber*, trans. M. Ilford (Allen Lane, The Penguin Press, London, 1968). Orig.: *Sociologie de Max Weber*, Presses Universitaire de France, Paris, 1966).

FROMM, E., *The Fear of Freedom* (Routledge & Kegan Paul, London, 1942:1960).

GELLNER, E., *Thought and Change* (Weidenfeld & Nicolson, London, 1964).
Words and Things (Gollancz & Penguin, London, 1959: 1963).

GOLEMBIEWSKI, R. T., and BLUMBERG, A., (Eds.) *Sensitivity Training and the Laboratory Approach* (Peacock Publishers, Inc., Illinois).

GORDON, W. J. J., *Synectics. The Development of Creative Capacity* (Evanston, New York and Harper & Row, London, 1961).

GOSLING, R., MILLER, D. H., TURQUET, P. M. and WOODHOUSE, D., *The Use of Small Groups in Training* (Codicote Press, 1967).

GUNTRIP, H., *Personality Structure & Human Interaction* (Hogarth Press, London, 1961).

HAMBLIN, C. L., *Elementary Formal Logic. A Programmed Course* (Methuen, London, 1966:1967).

HARE, A. P., BORGATTA, E. F. and BALES, R. F. (eds.), *Small Groups. Studies in Social Interaction* (Knopf, New York, 1955).

HARTMANN, H., *Essays on Ego Psychology* (Hogarth Press, London, 1964).

HEALTH, MINISTRY OF, *Psychiatric Nursing: Today & Tomorrow.* Central Health Services Council. Report of the Joint Sub-Committee of The Standing Mental Health and The Standing Nursing Advisory Committees. (H.M.S.O., London, 1968).

HEIDEGGER, MARTIN, *Being and Time* (Blackwell, 1967).

HERBST, P. G., *Autonomous Group Functioning. An Exploration in Behaviour Theory and Measurement* (Tavistock, London, 1962:1968).

HIRST, R. J. (ed.), *Philosophy. An Outline for the Intending Student* (Routledge & Kegan Paul, London, 1968).

HOME, H. J., *The Concept of Mind* (Int. J. Psycho-Anal. 1966, 47, 42–49).

HOPPER, E. (Editor), *Readings in the Theory of Educational Systems* (Hutchinson University Library, London, 1971).

HORNEY, K., *Our Inner Conflicts. A Constructive Theory of Neurosis* (Routledge & Kegan Paul, London, 1946).
Self-Analysis (Kegan Paul, Trench, Trubner, London, 1942).

HUIZINGA, J., *Homo Ludens. A Study of the Play Element in Culture* (Paladin, London, 1949:1970).

HUME, D., *On Human Nature & the Understanding*, ed. A. Flew (Collier Books, New York: Collier-Macmillan, London).

HUSSERL, E., *Cartesian Meditations*, trans. D. Cairns (Nijhoff, The Hague, 1960. Orig. in: *Husserliana*, 1950),
Ideas. General Introduction to Pure Phenomenology, trans.

W. R. Boyce Gibson (Allen & Unwin, London: Macmillan, New York, 1931. Orig.: *Ideen zu Einek Reinen Phänomenologie und Phänomenologischen Philosophie*, 1913). *The Idea of Phenomenology*, trans. W. P. Alston and G. Nakhnikian (Nijhoff, The Hague, 1964).

HUTTEN, E. H., *The Origins of Science* (Allen & Unwin, London, 1962).

INKELES, A., *What is Sociology?* (Prentice-Hall, Englewood Cliffs, N.J., 1964).

JASPERS, K., *General Psychopathology*, trans. J. Hoenig and M. W. Hamilton (Manchester U.P., Manchester, 1963).

JEANS, J., *Physics and Philosophy* (C.U.P., Cambridge, 1946).

JONES, M., *Social Psychiatry in Practice* (Penguin, London, 1968).

KADIS, A. L., KRASNER, J. D., WINICK, C. and FOULKES, S. H., *A Practicum of Group Psychotherapy* (Evanston, New York and Harper & Row, London, 1963).

KANT, I., *Critique of Pure Reason*, trans. F. M. Müller (New York, Doubleday Anchor, Garden City, 1966). *Prolegomena*, trans. P. G. Lucas (Manchester U.P., Manchester, 1953).

KATZ, D., *Gestalt Psychology*, trans. R. Tyson (Methuen, London, 1951).

KAUFMANN, W. (ed.), *Existentialism from Dostoevsky to Sartre* (Thames & Hudson, London, 1957).

KELLY, G. A., *A Theory of Personality. The Psychology of Personal Constructs* (Norton, New York, 1955:1963).

KING, M., *Heidegger's Philosophy* (Blackwell, Oxford, 1964).

KLAPMAN, J. W., *Group Psychotherapy. Theory and Practice* (Heinemann, London, 1946).

KLEIN, M., *Contributions to Psychoanalysis 1921–1945* (Hogarth Press, London, 1948). *The Psychoanalysis of Children*, trans. A. Strachey (Hogarth Press, London, 1949:1963. Orig. German Edition, 1932).

KÖHLER, W., *Gestalt Psychology* (Mentor, New York and Toronto, 1947).

KÖRNER, S., *Kant* (Penguin, London, 1955).

LAUER, Q., *Phenomenology. Its Genesis and Prospect* (Harper & Row, New York, 1965. Orig.: *The Triumph of Subjectivity*, 1958).

LAING, R. D., *The Politics of Experience and The Bird of Paradise* (Penguin, London, 1967). *The Self and Others. Further Studies in Sanity and Madness*. (Tavistock, London, 1961).

LAING, R. D. and COOPER, D. G., *Reason and Violence. A Decade of Sartre's Philosophy* (Tavistock Publications, London, 1964).

LAING, R. D. and ESTERSON, A., *Sanity, Madness and the Family* (Tavistock: Penguin, London, 1964:1970).

LEACH, E., *Lévi-Strauss* (Fontana/Collins, London, 1970).

LEDERMANN, E. K., *Philosophy and Medicine* (Tavistock Publications Ltd, 1970).

LEFEBVRE, H., *The Sociology of Marx*, trans. N. Guterman (Allen Lane, The Penguin Press, London, 1968. Orig: *Sociologie de Marx*, Presses Universitaires de France, Paris, 1966).

LÉVI-STRAUSS, C., *Structural Anthropology*, trans. C. Jacobson and B. G. Schoepf (Allen Lane, The Penguin Press, London, 1963:1968. Orig: *Anthropologie Structurale*, 1953).

   The Scope of Anthropology, trans. S. O. Paul and R. A. Paul (Cape, London, 1967).

LEWIN, K., *Field Theory in Social Science*, ed. D. Cartwright (Tavistock, London, 1952:1963).

   Resolving Social Conflicts. Selected Papers on Group Dynamics, ed. G. W. Lewin (Harper, New York, 1948).

LYONS, J., *Introduction to Theoretical Linguistics* (C.U.P., Cambridge, 1968).

LYONS, J. (ed.), *New Horizons in Linguistics* (Penguin, London, 1970).

MANDELBAUM, D. G. (ed.), 'Selected Writings of E. Sapir' in *Language, Culture & Personality* (University of California Press, Berkeley and Los Angeles, 1968).

MARTINDALE, D., *The Nature and Types of Sociological Theory* (Routledge & Kegan Paul, London, 1961).

MAY, R., *Psychology and The Human Dilemma* (Van Nostrand, Princeton, N.J., 1967).

   'The Existential Approach' in: *American Handbook of Psychiatry*, ed. S. Arieti. Vol. II. (Basic Books, New York, 1959).

MAY, R. (ed.), *Existential Psychology* (Random House, New York, 1961)

MAY, R., ANGEL, E. and BERG, H. F. E. (eds.), *Existence. A New Dimension in Psychiatry and Psychology* (Basic Books, New York, 1958).

McDOUGALL, W., *The Group Mind* (Putnam's, New York and London, 1920).

MEHTA, V., *Fly and the Fly-Bottle. Encounters with British Intellectuals* (Penguin, London, 1963:1965).

MELLONE, S. H., *Elements of Modern Logic* (University Tutorial Press, London, 1934:1966).

MILLER, G. A., *Psychology. The Science of Mental Life* (Hutchinson: Penguin, London, 1962:1966).

   'Psycholinguistics' in: *Handbook of Social Psychology*, ed. G. Linzey (Addison-Wesley, Reading, Mass. and London, 1954:1959).

   The Psychology of Communication (Allen Lane, The Penguin Press, London, 1968).

MOLINA, F., *Existentialism as Philosophy* (Prentice-Hall, Englewood Cliffs, N.J., 1962).

MORENO, J. L. (ed.), *Sociometry and The Science of Man* (Beacon House, New York, 1956).

MORENO, J. L., *Who Shall Survive?* (Beacon House, Inc., N.Y., 1953).

MULLAN, H. and ROSENBAUM, M., *Group Psychotherapy. Theory & Practice* (Free Press of Glencoe [Macmillan], New York, 1962).

MURPHY, G., *Psychological Thought from Pythagoras to Freud* (Harcourt, Brace, New York, 1968).

NAGEL, E., *The Structure of Science* (Routledge & Kegan Paul, London, 1961:1968).

NEEDLEMAN, J., *Being in the World* (Selected Papers of Ludwig Binswanger, Basic Books, 1963).

NEWCOMB, T. M., *Social Psychology* (Tavistock Publications, London, 1952).

ODAJNYK, W., *Marxism & Existentialism* (Doubleday, Anchor, Garden City, New York, 1965).

O'NEIL, W. M., *The Beginnings of Modern Psychology* (Penguin, London, 1968).

PEARS, D., *Wittgenstein* (Fontana/Collins, London, 1971).

PETERMAN, B., *The Gestalt Theory & The Problem of Configuration*, trans. M. Fortes (Routledge & Kegan Paul, London, 1932:1950).

POWDERMAKER, F. B. and FRANK, J. D., *Group Psychotherapy. Studies in Methodology of Research and Therapy*. Report of a Group Psychotherapy Research Project of the U.S. Veterans' Association, 1953.

RICE, A. K., *Learning for Leadership* (Tavistock Publications, London, 1965).

RICOEUR, P., *Freud and Philosophy. An Essay on Interpretation*, trans. D. Savage (Yale U.P., New Haven and London, 1970).

RIESMAN, D. with GLAZER, N. and DENNEY, R., *The Lonely Crowd. A Study of the Changing American Character* (Doubleday, Garden City, N.Y.).

ROHRER, J. H. and SHERIF, M. (eds.), *Social Psychology at the Crossroads* (Harper, New York).

ROSENBAUM, M. and BERGER, M. (eds.), *Group Psychotherapy and Group Function* (Basic Books Inc., 1963).

ROSS, D., *Aristotle* (Methuen, London; Barnes & Noble, New York, 1923:1949:1964).

ROYCE, J. R., *The Encapsulated Man. An Inter-Disciplinary Essay on the Search for Meaning* (Van Nostrand, Princeton, N.J., 1964).

RUESCH, J. and BATESON, G., *Communication. The Social Matrix of Psychiatry* (Norton & Co. Inc., 1951).

RUITENBEEK, H. M. (ed.), *Group Therapy Today. Styles, Methods & Techniques* (Atherton Press, New York, 1969).

RUNES, D. D. (ed.), *Dictionary of Philosophy* (Littlefield, Adams: Ames, Iowa, 1959).
Living Schools of Philosophy (Littlefield, Adams: Ames, Iowa, 1958. Orig: *20th Century Philosophy*, 1943).

RUSSELL, B., *History of Western Philosophy* (Allen & Unwin, London, 1946:1962).

RYCROFT, C., *A Critical Dictionary of Psychoanalysis* (Nelson, London, 1968).

RYCROFT, C. (ed.), *Psychoanalysis Observed* (Constable, London, 1966).

SARTRE, J.-P., *Existential Psychoanalysis*, trans. H. E. Barnes (Regnery, Chicago, 1953). A translation of a major section of *L'Etre et Le Néant*.
Existentialism & Humanism, trans. P. Mairet (1948:1957. Orig. *L'Existentialisme est un Humanisme*, 1946).
Nausea, trans. R. Baldick (1965. Orig. *La Nausée*, 1938).
The Problem of Method trans. H. E. Barnes (Methuen, London, 1963. Orig. *Question de Méthode*, in *Critique De La Raison Dialectique*, Paris, 1960).
The Transcendence of the Ego. An Existentialist Theory of Consciousness, trans. F. Williams and R. Kirkpatrick (Noonday Press, New York, 1957).

SCHULTZ, D. P., *Panic Behaviour* (Random House, New York, 1964).

SEGAL, H., *Introduction to the Work of Melanie Klein* (Heinemann, London, 1964).

SENFT, P., 'Uncertainty, Violence & Hope' (i) in *The Human Context*, August 1968 (Nijhoff, The Hague, 1968).

SILVERMAN, G., 'Research in Pathopsycholinguistics', Essay submitted for Mental Health Research Fund Registrar's Prize Competition. (?Unpublished, 1970).

SLAVSON, S. R., *A Textbook in Analytic Group Psychotherapy* (International Universities Press, New York, 1964).

SMITH, P. B. (ed.), *Group Processes. Selected Readings* (Penguin, London, 1970).

SPROTT, W. J. H., *Human Groups* (Penguin, London, 1958:1962).

STORR, A., *Human Aggression* (Allen Lane, The Penguin Press, London, 1968).

SYZ, H., *Reflections on Group – or Phylo-Analysis* (Acta psychother., Suppl., ad Vol. II: 37–88, 1963).

THÉVENAZ, P., *What is Phenomenology? And Other Essays*, trans. J. M. Edie (Quadrangle Books, Chicago, 1962).

THOMPSON, S. and KAHN, J. H., *The Group Process as a Helping Technique* (Pergamon Press, 1970).

THOMSON, R., *The Pelican History of Psychology* (Penguin, London, 1968).

TOULMIN, S., *The Philosophy of Science* (Hutchinson, London, 1953).

TROTTER, W., *Instincts of the Herd in Peace & War* (Ernest Benn, London, 1916:1930).

TUCKER, R. C., *Philosophy and Myth in Karl Marx* (C.U.P., Cambridge, 1961).

VERNON, J. A., *Inside the Black Room* (Penguin, London, 1963:1966).

VERSÉNYI, L., *Heidegger, Being and Truth* (Yale U.P., New Haven and London, 1965).

VICKERS, G., *Value Systems and Social Process* (Tavistock, London, 1968)

VON BERTALANFFY, L., *General System Theory* (George Braziller, 1968).

WANN, T. W. (ed.), *Behaviourism & Phenomenology* (University of Chicago Press, Chicago and London, 1964).

WATZLAWICK, P., BEAVIN, J. H. and JACKSON, D. D., *Pragmatics of Human Communication* (Faber & Faber, 1968).

WERTHEIMER, M., *Productive Thinking* (Tavistock Publications, London, 1961).

WHITAKER, D. S. and LIEBERMAN, M. A., *Psychotherapy through the Group Process* (Prentice-Hall Inc., 1964).

WHITEHEAD, A. N., *Science & the Modern World* (Mentor, New York and Toronto, 1925).

WIENER, N., *The Human Use of Human Beings* (Anchor Books, Doubleday, 1954).

WILLIAMS, R., *Communications* (Penguin, London, 1962:1963).

WILSON, C., *Introduction to the New Existentialism* (Hutchinson, London, 1966).

WITTGENSTEIN, L., *Philosophical Investigations*, trans. G. E. M. Abscombe (Blackwell, Oxford, 1953:1968).
    Tractatus Logico-Philosophicus. The German Text of *Logisch-Philosophische Abhandlung* with a trans, by D. F. Pears and B. F. McGuinness (Routledge & Kegan Paul, London, 1961:1966).

WOLF, A. and SCHWARTZ, E. K., *Psychoanalysis in Groups* (Grune & Stratton, New York, 1962).

WOODCOCK, G., *Anarchism. A History of Libertian Ideas & Movements* (Pelican, 1962).

YALOM, I. D., *The Theory and Practice of Group Psychotherapy* (Basic Books, New York and London, 1970).

Index

I.G.P.I., *see* Individual group psychological isomorphism
idealism, 24, 26, 29, 86
Illing, H., 50
individual group psychological isomorphism, 157
industrial psychology, 34–5, 39
Industrial Revolution, the, 22, 33
Infeld, L., 42
information theory, 179, *see also* cybernetics, communication theory
Institute of Psychoanalysis, the, 98
Instinct, 19, 169, i. theory, 107, 168, 169
intentionality, 113, 115, *see also* Husserl
intrapersonal processes, 135
Introduction to Group Therapy (Slavson), 64
Isolation and Psychotherapy (Camus & Pogniez), 47

Jackson, D., 154, 179
James, W., 30, 45, 53, 96, 98, 110
Jaspers, K., 15, 96, 121–2, 153, 163
Jesuits, the, 21
Johnson Abercrombie, M. L., 74
Jung, C. G., 28, 138, 169, and group therapy, 49–51, and Klein, 58, J., Freud and groups, 49–50, 58, cited by May, 97–8

Kant, I., 29, 85, 102, 109, 110, 111, and Sartre, 124
Kardiner, A., 26, 58–9
Kelly, G., 96
Kepler, J., 21, 95
Kierkegaard, S., 95, 106, 120–1
Klein, M., 54, 55, 57, 61, 74, 170, and Jung, 58, and Laing, 101
Koch, S., 115
Koffka, K., 80
Kohler, W., 80
koinonia, 189, *and see* One, the
Kraepelin, E., 43, 169
Kris, E., 56, 57
Kropotkin, P., 23, 63

La Salpêtrière, 47
Laing, R. D., 72, 96, 101–2, 124, 125, 154, and social phenomonology, 150, and Klein, 101
language, in Mead's theory, 33, and the revival-inspirational technique, 49, and mathematics, 85–6, and logical positivism, 94, 103–5, and phenomonology, 115, and Bernstein, 144–5, and socialization, 148
Laplace, P. S. de, 140
Lawrence, D. H., 62
Lazarus, 109
Lazell, E., 47–8, 71
Lebon, G., 31, 54
Leibnitz, G. W., 45, 81
Leviathan (Hobbes), 140

Lewin, K., 20, 40, 41–3, 61, 81, 153, and topological psychology, 80, and field theory, 120, 179, and Sartre, 125, and systems theory, 141, and Foulkes, 154–5, and psychoanalysis, 156–7, and T-groups, 72–3, 159, and group dynamics, 179, 185
Lieberman, M., 65–6, 158, 187
Lilienfeld, A. M., 141
Linton, R., 58
Lippitt, R., 40
Living Systems: Basic Concepts: Structure and Process: Cross Level Hypotheses. (Miller), 139
location, 177–178
Locke, J., 20, 23, 83, 85, 95, 112
Loewenstein, R. H., 57
logical positivism, 94, 103–6, 110, *see also* positivism
Lomas, P., 101
Lonely Crowd, The (Reisman), 36
Lorenz, K., 63
Lotze, R. H., 110
Luckman, T., 146–9
Luther, M., 120
Lyceum, the, 91

Macchiavelli, N., 26
Mach, E., 110
Machover, S., 71
macrofunctionalism-ists, 39–41, *see also* microfunctionalism
Malamud, D. I., 71
Manheim, K., 36
Marsh, C., 47–9, 71
Marx, K., 14, 40, 95, 124, and Comte, 25, and dialectical materialism, 28–9, 127–8, and Pythagoras, 89, and Sartre, 128–30, and cybernetics, 141, and socialization, 146
marxism, 38, 43, 59, 94, 125, 126, and social actionism, 36, and Sartre, 128, 130, and group psychotherapy, 129, and contradictions, 133, *see also* dialectical materialism
Marxism of J. P. Sartre, The (Desan), 124
Massachusetts Institute of Technology, 159
mathematics, 85–6, 103, 106, 114, 136–8
Matrix (see group matrix)
May, R., 78, 96, 97–8, 101
Mayo, E., 34–5, 39, 47
Mead, G. H., 32–3, 39, 60, 88, 141, 145, and structure, 142
Mead, M., 26, 58
'meaninglessness', 104–5
Merleau-Ponty, M., 108
Mesmer, A., 46
metacommunication, 134, 137, 151
microfunctionalism-ists, 35, 39–40, 60, 153, *see also* macrofunctionalism, group dynamics
metastructure, 18, 161